A Healing HAVEN

Saving Horses and Humans at RVR Horse Rescue

Shirley Alarie

As told by Shawn Jayroe et al.

A Healing Haven
Saving Horses and Humans at RVR Horse Rescue
All Rights Reserved.
Copyright © 2015 Shirley Alarie
v1.0

Cover Photos © 2015 RVR Horse Rescue. Photographers Karen Pack, Catey Kuzma, and Shawn Hooper. All rights reserved – used with permission.

To Mom and my RVR Angels,
None of this would have been possible without you.
—Shawn

. . .

To Shawn,
You are an incredible inspiration and I am honored to
call you my friend.
—Shirley

TABLE OF CONTENTS

CHAPTER 1

I heard her sobbing before the phone even reached my ear.

"Hello," I said.

"Somebody gave me your number and said that you could help! They say you rescue horses . . ." The lady struggled to speak through her tears.

"Yes," I answered. "How can I help you?"

The caller hesitated. "My neighbors were running barrels with this really skinny horse. They hurt him badly. . . . I'm afraid they'll harm my horses if they find out that I called you, so I need to stay anonymous." She was torn between doing the right thing and the repercussions it might mean for her.

"We'll figure something out," I assured her. "What happened?"

"They were running barrels with him in the middle of the day—in one-hundred-degree heat! They had other horses out there running, too, but this one collapsed. He couldn't get up so they started whipping and beating him to make him get out of the way. He couldn't! They got their stupid redneck truck and tied ropes around his feet and dragged him out to the backfield to die. He's still out there! . . . He's out there dying." The Good Samaritan was devastated.

The strenuous sport of riding a horse at high speeds not to mention tight turns around barrels is taxing to even the healthiest horses, and the horse she was describing was far from healthy.

"There's also a pony out there that they are very mean to . . . I can't stand it anymore. The part that kills me is, I sold them the horse," she continued.

"Ma'am, can you go buy him back?" I suggested.

"I don't have any money, and I don't have the means to fix him," the desperate woman replied.

"Have you called the sheriff's department?" I asked her.

"Yes," she cried. "Lots of times. I told them I didn't want the neighbor to know who reported him. They never do anything as long as there's food and water on the property! The police in this city just don't care!"

"Well, if you buy him back, I will reimburse you when we pick him up. Will that work for you?" I offered.

Based on the plan, the Good Samaritan offered the abusive neighbor $100 to buy the horse back, and requested that the pony be included. The neighbor accepted.

I dispatched our Rescue Angels for the long trek to bring home the newest members of the ranch: Stormy, the horse, and Biscuit, the pony.

On September 24, 2010, at 11:30 a.m., Michelle and Matt arrived to pick up Stormy and Biscuit, and Stormy's nightmare was finally over. In near-death condition, Stormy rushed into the trailer in a desperate attempt to flee his tormenters. He seemed to understand that the newly arrived strangers with the trailer represented an escape.

The two-hour trip back to the ranch proved to be too taxing for his frail condition and Stormy collapsed immediately after exiting the trailer. There lay this beautiful white Arabian— dirty, sweaty, and bloody. A raggedy pile of skin and bones.

The vet was waiting on site in anticipation of their arrival. Stormy remained still during his examination. The doctor's initial assessment wasn't promising, confirming my initial guess, and I considered ending his misery on the spot.

In the horse world, we say that our beloved equines cross the "Rainbow Bridge" when they pass away. The phrase comes from a poem inspired by a Norse legend. There are several variations, but one version goes as follows.

By the edge of a woods, at the foot of a hill,
Is a lush, green meadow where time stands still.
Where the friends of man and woman do run,
When their time on earth is over and done.
For here, between this world and the next,
Is a place where each beloved creature finds rest.
On this golden land, they wait and they play,
Till the Rainbow Bridge they cross over one day.
No more do they suffer, in pain or in sadness,
For here they are whole, their lives filled with
gladness.
Their limbs are restored, their health renewed,
Their bodies have healed, with strength imbued.
They romp through the grass, without even a care,
Until one day they start, and sniff at the air.
All ears prick forward, eyes dart front and back,
Then all of a sudden, one breaks from the pack.
For just at that instant, their eyes have met;
Together again, both person and pet.
So they run to each other, these friends from long
past,
The time of their parting is over at last.
The sadness they felt while they were apart,
Has turned into joy once more in each heart.
They embrace with a love that will last forever,
And then, side-by-side, they cross over . . .
together.
(Steve and Diane Bodofsky, "The Rainbow
Bridge")

I had helped my share of horses cross the Rainbow Bridge
in my years of horse rescue, but I couldn't stand the thought that
Stormy would die under such deplorable circumstances at the

hands of humans. I was determined to show him the love and care he deserved. And so, I authorized the vet to administer painkillers and antibiotics to begin Stormy's fight for life.

His abusive owners had pushed him beyond his limits, to the point that the suspensory ligaments in his leg were torn and caused him to collapse, which was the incident the Good Samaritan had witnessed. The ropes they had tied to his legs to drag him had nearly severed one hoof and caused considerable damage to another. Being dragged behind the truck had scraped and scratched his side.

Telltale wounds of repeated beatings were in various stages of healing. An ill-fitting saddle had torn his back and sides. The green, oozing, inflamed infections on Stormy's ankles conveyed an unspoken story of evil torture and neglect.

The vet was enraged at the condition of his stricken patient. After his assessment, he recommended I file for a criminal investigation and even offered to testify to the heinous treatment made evident by the severity of Stormy's afflictions.

His abusers had literally run him into the ground, but his life had just taken an amazing turn with his rescue. Stormy was mine now, and I was determined not to give up on him.

Among U.S. states, the 2007 American Horse Council report put Texas in the lead with 978,822 horses, followed by California with 698,345, and Florida with 500,124.[1]

CHAPTER 2

Although I was born in Minnesota, I have lived everywhere. My father was an incredibly savvy and adaptable business dynamo. He found success in the Texas oil industry, at his mortgage lending company, and as an independent motivational speaker for the sales teams of large corporations. We moved to wherever Dad's latest business adventure led us. His intellect and shrewd business skills helped him bounce back each time an opportunity faltered. His affiliation with Muhammad Ali ultimately brought us to Tampa, Florida, but our roots always remained planted in Texas.

My mom was amazing in her own right; she shattered the mold of the traditional woman's role for her era. She pursued her dreams, even when they clashed with societal norms. She obtained a contractor's license, became a recreational airplane pilot and worked toward a commercial license, and rode a motorcycle—all accomplishments that were considered atypical for a woman in the 1960s. Her zest for life and motivation inspired me.

I cherished any time spent with my mom, but my most treasured memory is the thrill of tearing through the sky in one of the family planes. When viewed from the heavens, the green

---

[1] DVM360. "U.S. has 9.5 million horses, most in world, report says." October 1, 2007. http://veterinarynews.dvm360.com/us-has-95-million-horses-most-world-report-says (accessed 8/22/15).

and brown rectangles, separated by a maze of gray meandering roads, seemed like a foreign world.

I begged Mom to perform her twirls and loops and all the tricks she knew, like the "touch and go," where she would command the wheels to gently graze the ground before soaring immediately into the air again. I felt alive and free as we performed acrobatic dances in our aerial playground. I couldn't get enough of it, whereas my brother hovered over his barf bag in the backseat, hoping his Dramamine would take effect.

Our home base was TE Mercer Ranch, a thousand-acre cattle ranch in Fort Worth. Mexican immigrants worked the cattle, and I became fluent in Spanish after befriending their children.

Huge pillars stood guard at the entrance of the property while a recessed cattle guard spanned the opening. Sunken metal rods spaced several inches apart deterred the animals from escaping, while allowing humans to pass unimpeded. A lengthy driveway cut through the pasture our horses shared with the cattle. It ended at our home, which was enclosed by a fence to separate our yard from the surrounding pasture.

The house was a beautiful, sprawling Southern mansion, situated near the center of the estate. Each of the fourteen bedrooms was accompanied by its own sitting room. The fireplace in my bedroom was functional, but it was more decorative than useful during the mild Texas winters.

Our two Cessna planes transported us to any location that suited my parents' fancy. Whether it be for dining or shopping or sightseeing, no outing was too small to warrant aerial transportation.

When I was seven or eight years old, my father surprised me with my first horse at River Ranch in Tampa. We named him Ringo Starr and had him transported to Texas, where he and I bonded immediately. Ours was a loving and trusting connection.

Ringsin, as we called him, would run to greet me when I approached. I rode him everywhere without a bridal or saddle. Bareback, just me and my boy. We'd ride all over the property without a particular destination, simply enjoying the magical connection only possible between horse and rider. In the morning, he'd kneel down so I could climb aboard for a ride across the grounds to the bus stop at the highway. He'd spend the day grazing near the road while waiting for me to return from school. Then he'd carry me back to the house in blissful harmony.

Over time, Ringsin and I became rodeo junkies. After racing for competition, we'd entertain the audience during our intermission shows, where we performed pole bending and other circus-type tricks. My boy was a crowd-pleaser and did anything I asked of him. He'd lie down, rear up and sit, and roll over like a dog.

My early life was a fairytale of sorts, except the enchanted facade disguised a troubled reality. The lavish lifestyle we enjoyed was dampened by my father's temper, which was normally unleashed at my mother. The incredible strength she showed in all other areas of her life was sorely missing when it came to defending herself. She stayed in the marriage, believing it was in the best interest of her children.

As an impressionable child, I was left with permanent scars. The drama around my parents cemented my fierce protection of my mother, the underdog. I compensated for my mother's tolerance with rebellion, challenging my father's anger with my own.

Dad provided extravagant gifts, such as Ringo Starr, as an apology for all the turmoil. But none of his material bribery ever mattered to me. The only thing I longed for was his love.

My childhood was one of the best times of my life, but it was spattered with such mayhem and pain that when I was eighteen years old and Mom finally decided to divorce Dad, I followed her and my brothers out of town.

Escaping from that environment was like shedding dead weight I had been lugging around for too many years. The experience had altered my DNA, and I became resolute in my mission to protect the underdog. Once I found my voice, no one would ever stop me.

CHAPTER 3

After my parents' divorce, Mom hauled my brothers to a familiar but distant location. I joined them in Tampa, but maintained my own independence and quickly realized that the lavish traditions we enjoyed at Mercer Ranch were not that of the typical American lifestyle. The average Joe didn't hop in his plane to explore some far-off destination after school. However, wealth had come to represent a dark coffin that suffocated me, and I was anxious to start over. The scars of my childhood followed me into adulthood, refusing to remain behind as much as I tried to shed them like an irritating scratchy wool sweater.

I spread my own wings with nothing in my wallet but sheer determination and will to succeed. Drugs and alcohol lured me into their world, and there I found a man with similar interests. Beyond partying, we had little in common but I found myself pregnant nonetheless.

I straightened out my act as a new mom and began to walk the straight and narrow path as a parent. I carved a hard, firm line when it came to being mistreated, and that included the dysfunction that walks hand in hand with alcoholism. My

---

[2] American Horse Council. "State Breakout Studies." www.horsecouncil.org/state-breakout-studies-following-states (accessed 8/22/15).

precious daughter, Dee Dee, would not be raised amid chaos, so I ventured out on my own with my baby girl in tow.

I was stumbling along a rocky path in my personal life, but kicking ass professionally. I began my journey at cosmetology school in Tampa and fulfilled my dream of becoming a hairdresser. Cutting and styling hair satisfied my creative nature. And there may have been some tiny nugget tucked deep inside of me that smirked at the thought of bucking my father's desires for my future. A part of me continued to rebel against him, even though I was no longer under his influence.

My cosmetology certification earned me entry into a little salon, where I hustled seven days a week to eke out a living for Dee Dee and myself. Slowly my reputation grew. Devoted clientele followed me when I moved to a couple of different shops.

My life was dedicated to raising my daughter and building my career, until Dale entered the picture and proved to be a loving father figure to Dee Dee, which endeared him to me all the more. When I later became pregnant with Breena, Dale and I married.

Dale was a good man. His role as a stay-at-home father allowed me to continue to hone my hair-styling skills. However, the responsibility of parenting hadn't convinced him to curb his adolescent partying, and his repeated promises that he would stop proved to be empty lies. The cracks from this wedge quickly drove our union apart.

He was a weight chained to my ankles rather than a partner who could share my dreams. He pulled backward as determinedly as I pushed forward, and after five years our marriage crumbled.

I struggled like any single mom to hold our world together when every seam had busted apart. I wanted my children to maintain a relationship with Dale, but wouldn't tolerate regular or extended visits because of the alcoholism that continued to plague him. My way to ensure I maintained control over their contact with him was to refuse any child support, a decision that may have been influenced by my staunch independence. Still, that choice forced me to work even harder to provide for my children's needs.

My work as a hairstylist proved extremely rewarding. Not only did I enjoy the creative aspect, but I found the atmosphere itself provided a mental escape. The buzz of the shop was electric. Entering through those doors was like stepping into an entertaining soap opera starring unforgettable characters. But best of all, I fit in there.

As in any business, the good was accompanied by hassle. I became increasingly disgruntled with the petty backstabbing and other practices that I felt undermined the stylists. In response, I decided to open my own shop. By that time, I had dedicated clientele and enough experience that I felt confident I could manage the business. I launched Hair Perfections in 1985 with three chairs, a line of skincare products, wigs, hair braiding, and a dream.

Running the business as a single parent was challenging, but the overwhelming burden lifted when I hired an assistant, Richard. Besides being a talented stylist, he clicked with me, and our relationship quickly blossomed into a friendship of a lifetime.

I was a desperately lonely and struggling. My mother had moved out of town with her new man, Frank, leaving me to raise my daughters alone. I'd written off men after two failed relationships, but Richard was my sunshine. He lifted the loneliness, filled the void, and fueled me with strength to keep forging forward.

Owning the shop allowed me the flexibility to juggle being a parent with being a bread winner. I rolled with the punches and simply did my very best, but sometimes even sincere intentions don't produce the desired result. In retrospect, my fierce protection of the kids bordered on being overprotective, and my daughters struggled, particularly the older Dee Dee.

I bounced her from one school to another, searching for an evasive answer that never came. Her gravitational pull was always to the wrong crowd. Private school resulted in the same outcome. Finally, I bought her a horse, and that helped for the time being.

By this time, I had turned Richard loose at the salon and he rocked like a superstar. Hair Perfections was booming and my girls were old enough to join me at the shop. By their teens, they had learned how to do shampoos and other basic functions. They staved off boredom by hanging out with the son of a fellow business owner, staying occupied by tossing a football and playing other games. The shop was our home away from home.

It was a constant juggling act to prevent all my balls from crashing to the ground. I gave everything I had to my kids and my career, but I often felt that my best still wasn't good enough. Sometimes it seems that the pot of gold at the end of the rainbow called the American Dream keeps moving just out of reach, but I wouldn't stop trying.

Each year in the United States, an estimated 7 million people ride horses.[3]

CHAPTER 4

My childhood passion for horses followed me into adulthood. As chaotic as life became at times, there was always room for the majestic beauties that brought me great peace.

One of the perks of my wealthy childhood was my involvement in rodeos. Ringsin and I had perfected our intermission show and performed to receptive audiences that appreciated our fancy tricks. Our endless hours of training and preparation served to cement my deep love for Ringsin, as well as my devotion to horses in general.

As cherished as my memories from the rodeo were, it was there that I first witnessed the darker side of horsemanship. The animals were often treated as inanimate vehicles rather than beings with feelings. Unconscionable whippings and beatings sickened me. I couldn't fathom how an owner could or would treat a horse so barbarically. Those experiences etched an everlasting impression that haunted me into adulthood.

When I ventured out on my own, I would board my current horse at various facilities and observe other animals and their living conditions. Too often I observed mistreatment.

At one farm, horses were rented out for daily trail rides, known as hacklines. The customers rode horses without supervision, which precluded the owner of the facility from knowing whether the horses had been treated well or poorly.

---

[3] Riders4Helmets. "Statistics and Facts." www.riders4helmets.com/equestrians/ (accessed 8/22/15).

One day I witnessed a woman break a branch off a tree and proceed to beat the horse she was riding, and I snapped. My normally introverted nature was overtaken by seething anger and I couldn't keep quiet.

"Hey, the saddle is wrong and that's why she's not going," I lied to the lady.

"Really?" she asked.

"Yeah, get off and I'll fix it for you," I told her.

She dismounted so I could resolve the problem.

"Oh, this bit is not fitting her right either," I fibbed again. I took the bridal off, draped it over the horn of the saddle, then swatted the horse on the butt, which was her signal to return to the barn. She fled without hesitation.

"Walk back," I sneered at the obnoxious brat, who stared at me in disbelief.

Then and there, I decided to help defenseless abused horses. Once I set my mind to something, it generally happened, and I was determined to make a difference.

After that incident, I was so disgusted that I moved my horse to another barn, but returned two months later to check on the mare I had seen mistreated. Kids were riding her and I could see she was in pain, but the inexperienced children were oblivious to it. Dirt darkened her neglected gray coat and I had to act.

Everything is for sale for the right price, and after a quick exchange with the owner, the horse, named Lady, was mine. I forked over the $900 to seal the deal, then moved my new girl to the ranch where I boarded my current horse. I found that Lady's bursitis and terrible sores were the source of her suffering. The vet estimated she couldn't be ridden for a year so that her taxed body could be given an opportunity to heal.

I gave Lady to Dee Dee both to support her through a rough adolescence and to give Lady the love and care she deserved. As a typical preteen, Dee Dee enjoyed riding, but wasn't as enthusiastic about the grooming and upkeep required.

"You're not a good horse owner," I finally told her after she ran out of chances. "I'm finding Lady a new home."

Harsh? Maybe. But my standards for horse care are unwavering, even for my family.

My shop was the perfect venue for networking. Customers churning through a revolving door allowed me to reach an expansive audience, so I floated the message: Lady needed a home.

One of my regular patrons competed in dressage, the equestrian sport of highly specialized coordinated movements of a horse and rider. She expressed a potential interest in Lady, then came to evaluate her soundness and temperament. To our amazement and delight, Lady performed dressage moves magically. It saddened me that such a highly trained performer ended up on a hackline, but she found her way into a loving home and resides with the woman to this day.

Lady was my first foray into the world of rescue, and with that taste, I wanted more. I made rounds of the local boarding ranches and observed the horses there, stepping in when I felt there was a need. I transported my rescues to the barn where I boarded the rest of my horses and they remained there, under my care, while I found them new homes through my growing network.

I became known for my love of horses, the rescues I had begun rehoming, and my dream to launch a full-fledged rescue facility. My method of housing the rescues temporarily at boarding facilities was effective but expensive. I could manage a couple of horses at one time, but there were many more in need. I couldn't make a significant difference without my own facility. I needed land.

One of my customers owned property and approached me about the possibility of buying it from him. The spot was a perfect match for my vision, as it already had several stalls, but I quickly realized that there was just no way to swing it. Raising two children was my top priority. I had to pass on his offer, but our discussions had triggered a smoldering idea that begged to be ignited.

In the meantime, my shop continued to grow in popularity and business flourished. I was enjoying life and living comfortably. My horse rescue efforts were picking up momentum and I could more easily afford the boarding costs in addition to building up wealth of my own.

The girls and I moved into an upscale neighborhood in Temple Terrace, near the shop. The enormous lanai enclosed the pool as well as a private garden oasis and outdoor bar for entertaining. It was a far cry from Mercer Ranch, but the fruits of my hard work were ripening.

After providing well for my daughters and the horses, I decided to grant myself one self-indulgence. Corvettes had always been my love. I owned a collection of various signature paraphernalia, but it was time for the real deal, and not just any old Vette would do. A bright red T-top was the only way to go. Standard transmission, of course.

I felt alive and free as I zipped around town in my shiny new 2003 wheels. Oh yeah, I was making it.

> *Seven equestrian disciplines vie in international competitions: jumping, dressage, eventing, reining, vaulting, endurance, and driving. Polo and rodeo competition also fall in the spirited equestrian category.*[4]

CHAPTER 5

Equestrian sports originated over two thousand years ago when the Greeks introduced dressage, a highly regimented training program to prepare their horses for war. [5] Later, during the Middle Ages, cooperative effort between horse and rider further developed with the introduction of the three-day event, also known as eventing. This triathlon consists of the original Greek dressage, plus cross country and show jumping. Dressage requires a specific sequence of movements, whereas cross country demonstrates physical endurance and trust between horse and rider while clearing obstacles. Lastly, show jumping tests the technical jumping skills of the horse and rider. Each of these three facets would prepare horse and soldier for situations they might encounter during war.

In time, the same practices evolved into competitive sports as we know them today. The extensive training required to attain the superior skill, cooperation, and trust between human and horse earned them entry as prestigious Olympic sporting events.

[4] Sports Destination Management. "Equestrian Sports Beyond Racing." June 30, 2010 www.sportsdestinations.com/sports/equestrian/equestrian-sports-beyond-racing-4614 (accessed 8/22/15).
[5] Wikipedia. "Horses in warfare." https://en.wikipedia.org/wiki/Horses_in_warfare (accessed 8/22/15).

Over the years, numerous other equestrian sports also evolved. Some are competitive in nature and some are not. In any case, the cooperation between horse and rider is often a beautiful bonding experience. However, sometimes the human's desire to win competitive events may lead to abuse of the animal. The value of a prize, or merely competition itself, can supersede humane treatment.

One sporting horse prone to abuse is the Tennessee Walking Horse.[6] In 1939, the first Tennessee Walking Horse National Celebration was held to showcase the exaggerated, high-stepping "running walk" gait of these good-natured beauties. The competitive nature of the event led to a cruel practice known as soring. If bearing weight on a horse's foot causes him pain, he will lift the leg quickly once his foot touches the ground. Soring ensures that the horse will be in pain when he bears weight on his foot, therefore raising it quickly and creating the desired gait, known as the Big Lick. This barbaric practice involves either cutting, or applying pressure or chemicals to the horse's feet and legs to inflict intentional pain. The addition of tall heavy shoes, comparable to women's stiletto heels, magnifies the gait while adding additional discomfort.

Humane organizations have rallied to end this abusive practice, imploring the sporting enthusiasts to enjoy the magnificence of the naturally trained Tennessee Walking Horses instead. Although soring is now illegal, it still occurs occasionally.

One of my first ventures into the horse rescue world was with a Tennessee Walker named Sassy. My horse networking had just started to gain momentum and people who knew of my interest began feeding me information about horses in need. The

[6] Wikipedia. "Tennessee Walking Horse." https://en.wikipedia.org/wiki/Tennessee_Walking_Horse (accessed 8/22/15).

day that Sassy's story was brought to my attention, I decided to act.

She was being boarded at a facility east of Tampa, near Brandon. Under the guise of a potential customer, I visited the ranch a few times to check out the conditions. Each time I toured the facility, there was one horse always in her stall, standing in mud. The pretty black mare would come to greet me when I walked past her. I asked the ranch owner if they ever let her out.

"She's fine," he told me. "Her owner is old and doesn't come around much, so she's in her stall most of the time."

Not satisfied with that answer or with the observations I'd made, I decided to board my horse there so I could keep a close eye on the imprisoned girl. I fell in love with her over the course of our meetings.

I offered to buy Sassy, and although her owner was happy to relinquish her, it wouldn't be cheap. I ended up paying a steep $8,000 to free her. Once she was mine, I removed her clunky block shoes, thereby returning her to her natural state. With this freedom, she ran and ran and ran and ran. It was the most beautiful sight to witness her run wild and pain-free.

At the time, I was in the middle of a move, so I temporarily boarded Sassy and my other horse at my friend Ray's place. I intended to move the horses to their final destination once I was settled and found another suitable facility near my new home.

Ray was a devoted caretaker, showering the pair with time and attention, and spoiling them with treats. Sassy's growing attachment to Ray was evident when she started running to greet him at the fence when he'd come home. Soon their bond solidified into a deep mutual love.

When I was ready to retrieve my horses after the move, I loaded them into the trailer, but Sassy wanted no part of it and proceeded to throw a fit. Her pathetic screams shredded my heart.

How could I tear her from the man she clearly loved? Even though I loved Sassy, she loved Ray, and there was no way I could take her away from him—not after the pain and suffering she had already endured. In Sassy's best interest, I returned her to her beloved Ray and they still reside together to this day.

I had assumed that answering my horse rescue calling would bring me great joy as well as incredible sadness. Sassy's rescue confirmed that I had been right; this journey would include both pleasure and pain, and I had only just begun.

From earliest times, rare white horses have been mythologized as possessing exceptional properties, transcending the normal world by having wings (e.g., Pegasus from Greek mythology) or horns (the unicorn).[7]

CHAPTER 6

On the religious front, I have always known there is a God. In fact, I'm still certain of it. Mom was Christian, but didn't want to impose her views on her children. Instead, she dropped off my brothers and me for services at various religious denominations so we could experience the differences and choose for ourselves.

God awaited me in every church, but I never associated Him with a particular religious sect. In my early twenties, I accepted the Lord as my Savior at Bethel Temple in Tampa, an experience that filled me with unspeakable and inexplicable joy.

Unfortunately I later became enticed by the demons of partying and every other vice that I considered to be "having a good time." I swept Jesus out of my mind while living life by my own agenda. Alcohol, depression, financial problems, two failed relationships, divorce, and parenting challenges not only led me to stray from God but also led me to write off any notion of a romantic relationship. I lugged around monumental baggage.

I didn't need a man in my life, but ironically, Richard and I became inseparable. As my salon assistant, he was the one man I allowed into my world. We were peanut butter and jelly for twelve years—we even lived together— and created an ironclad bond that never extended beyond platonic.

[7] Wikipedia. "White horse (mythology)." https://en.wikipedia.org/wiki/White_horse_(mythology) (accessed 8/22/15).

On April Fool's Day in 2001, Richard and I spent the day dropping money at several shops around town, returning home later in the afternoon. We tossed our bags of goodies on the table and hunkered down for a relaxing evening of dinner and television.

Around three o'clock in the morning, I was awakened by Richard in my room. Sobbing over his agonizing headache, he plopped down on the bed, clutching and pulling at me in desperation for some help I could not offer him. He stood back up and passed out.

I called 911 and he was rushed by ambulance to the hospital, while I followed in my car. When they removed him from the ambulance, I stood in shock and horror. A green plastic manual resuscitator was now the only thing standing between my friend and death. The first-responders pumped life-saving air into my friend's lungs as they whisked him inside.

The doctor confirmed a brain aneurism had left Richard with a measly 15 percent chance of survival. Assuming he pulled through the emergency surgery, he would most likely remain a vegetable.

Upon hearing Richard's dismal prognosis, I decided to take care of him for the rest of his life. I had no idea how I was going to do it, but I was committed. Every scenario raced through my mind while I waited on pins and needles during his surgery.

He survived the operation, overcoming the initial hurdle, but he remained on life support for the next five days. I was glued to his side, consumed with worry. Until I knew he would be alright, I couldn't eat, drink, or sleep.

My only ventures from Richard's bedside were to the chapel where I pleaded with God not to take my dear friend from this world. I even tried to strike up a deal. I begged, "I will come back to you and go to church regularly if you just let him live. Please don't take him. He's my only friend in the world."

Upon returning from one bartering session in the chapel, I found a yellow sticky note at the edge of Richard's bed. It read, "For I know the plans I have for you," from Jeremiah 29:11 in the Bible.

I didn't know who left the note for Richard but I folded it up and stuffed it in my pocket so it wouldn't fall off and get lost.

In the days following it became clear that Richard wasn't going to make it. My original pleas for his life to be spared were replaced with prayers for strength to handle his passing. I needed all the help I could get since I have a history of fainting at the sight of blood and suffering, let alone death. Even a routine doctor or dental procedure can trigger a bout. Shortly before Richard got sick, a kidney infection landed my daughter in the emergency room and I passed out while calming her during the blood draw.

Knowing my low tolerance, I prayed for the fortitude I would need as my friend approached his death. I didn't understand why I hadn't paled once during the medical crisis that unraveled before me or how I had maintained incredible stamina without nourishment or sleep.

I knew when it was time for Richard to go. I was sitting next to his bed, holding his hand. "Your angels are waiting for you, Richard. They are here to walk you into your next life," I whispered, giving him permission to leave this world.

And with that, he was gone. At only thirty-four years old, my precious friend was dead.

My wall of strength crumbled and I collapsed into hysterics as I hugged him and said good-bye. My heart was broken, yet overflowing at the fact that he had waited for my approval to let go.

The nurses escorted me into a quiet room where I pieced myself back together. Out of the silence, a distinct voice came from nowhere. "It's okay, you can go home now. It's okay," it said.

At the time I thought it was Richard, but I know now it was God speaking directly to me and pulling me back to Him during this tragedy. He had been my strength, the source of my stamina when my body lacked the sustenance it needed. He carried me when I needed him most, even though I walked away from Him so many years ago. Tragedy turns some people away from religion, but I was blessed that Richard's crisis led me straight back.

Next came the task of planning the funeral. Richard's family wanted an open casket and I panicked. My friend had been beyond vain about his hair and paranoid at the thought that it might be thinning. During the emergency surgery, his head was shaved completely. Richard would have been mortified to be bald, and more so at the idea of his family, friends, and customers seeing him for the first and final time that way. I had to do something fast.

I rushed to Custom Hair, a wig shop in Tampa, but it was Monday and they were closed. A cleaning team scurried around inside the locked doors. I knocked and begged them to let me in, but it was to no avail. I pled my case into the crack between the door and its frame, explaining my friend's wake was that evening and he needed hair. Even an offer of $500 failed to convince them.

The bewildered cleaners explained that the shop was closed and they didn't have the authority to let me in. Heartbroken, I laid down in front of the glass doors and all my grief, anger, and frustration boiled over and sprinkled onto the sidewalk. Sometime later I saw one of the cleaning women on her phone and I assumed she was calling the police. However, my resolve was rewarded when one of them opened the door. The shop owner had shown mercy on me and would allow me to get what I needed. I grabbed a wig the same color as Richard's hair and the owner walked the cleaning lady through the credit card sale over the phone.

The price was steep, but I didn't care. I had hair for my buddy's head. My next challenge would be turning a woman's wig into Richard's haircut. I hurried to make the thirty miles to the funeral home before the guests started arriving for the wake. There was no time to spare.

When I arrived at the funeral home, there was only one man there. He led me into a frigid and eerily quiet dark room, then flipped on a dull light. There lay my best friend as though he were sleeping. Once I was situated, the man retreated, leaving me alone with Richard's body.

Knowing I was short on time, I pulled out my scissors, combs, and hairspray. How was I going to do this? I had never seen a dead person before, let alone someone I loved.

I slid down the side of his casket as another wave of grief washed over me. I cried for strength to accomplish my mission and make this fake hair look real.

Even as an experienced stylist, I'd never cut that type of hairpiece before. I stood over Richard while holding the newly purchased hair and wondered how I would start. I lifted his cold, stiff, shaven head with one hand and pulled the wig over it with the other.

Once I began working, I fell into a zone and determination replaced my tears. I was an artist, whittling the bushy mop into Richard's haircut. I snipped one way and then the other. Bit by bit, each cut began to fall together like magic.

When I stood back to check my work, I couldn't believe my eyes. I was certain Richard would have been pleased with the end result and it felt like I had just performed a miracle.

*The horse is a universal symbol of freedom
without restraint, because riding a horse
made people feel they could free themselves
from their own bindings.*[8]

CHAPTER 7

In the days following Richard's death, I slumped around at the house that was becoming more cluttered with each passing day. Although I still felt crappy, I finally started pulling myself together and putting my place back in order. I picked up a bag that had been dropped on the dining room table after Richard and I returned from our last shopping excursion. Inside, I found a turtle. It was the ceramic figurine I had considered buying to add to my collection around my pond in the lanai. After checking the price, I decided against the purchase, but Richard must have snuck back to buy it. While holding the sweet final physical connection to my dear friend, I felt he was telling me, "It's okay. Stop crying. I'm with you."

Richard's funeral was scheduled for a couple days after the wake. Another close friend had offered to give the eulogy, to my great relief. There was no way I could give it and the family members were too heartbroken, so it was a blessing that he had stepped up.

At midnight, the night before the funeral, Richard's friend called. He wouldn't be able to attend, so I would have to give the eulogy after all. He emailed me the notes he had written so I could read what he prepared.

---

[8] Pure Spirit. "Horse Symbolism." www.pure-spirit.com/more-animal-symbolism/232-pure-spirit-minneapolis-st-paul-dog-training-and-international-all-species-animal-communication-horse-symbolism (accessed 8/22/15).

However, while reading the notes, my heart dropped. It consisted mostly of hard to read poems; there was barely any mention of Richard. There was no way I could pull it off and it only served to trigger another round of tears.

By this time it was one o'clock in the morning. I turned to the Lord with another request. "Help me find the right words to say," I prayed. Sure enough, when I started to write, the words flowed perfectly and I was back in bed by two o'clock.

I was a jittery wreck as I prepared for the funeral. Speaking in front of a large group of people is generally the last place you would ever find me. But that's exactly where I ended up when it was time for my speech. Before I began, I turned heavenward once again. "In Jesus's name I pray that you would give me the strength to do this."

My tribute to Richard poured out beautifully. The funeral director said it was one of the most lovely and well put together eulogies he had ever heard. I had the audience laughing and crying as together we fondly reminisced through Richard's short life. It was a remarkable experience and I was honored to present the final tribute for my friend.

The day after the funeral, I had to return to work and I was dreading it. Richard had amassed a huge clientele in the twelve years that he and I had worked side by side. There had only been three of us in the salon, and the third person didn't really know Richard, which meant I would be the one deluged with questions.

In anticipation, I wrote a thirty-page letter to Richard's friends and clients, again with God's guidance to find just the right words. I made one thousand copies at Office Depot and, rather than having to constantly rehash raw memories, I would hand a letter to anyone who asked about Richard.

The morning I was to return to work for the first time without Richard, I stared at my reflection in the bathroom mirror as I applied my makeup. Pain from my loss overflowed, leaving a mess of black streaks and smudges on my cheeks in its wake. I couldn't face all those people so soon.

A pile of money and other pocket-junk I collected while Richard was in the hospital was scattered on the counter in front of me. Amid the jumble, I spotted the folded yellow sticky note that had been left for Richard at the foot of his bed. It was peeking out from beneath the spare coins.

I unfolded it and read it again. "For I know the plans I have for you." What plans? Richard's dead. What plans can there be for him?

"For I know the plans I have for you, says the Lord. They are plans for good and not for evil, to give you a future and a hope. In those days when you pray, I will listen. You will find me when you seek me, if you look for me in earnest."[9]

DING, DING, DING . . . The note hadn't been for Richard . . . It was for *me!*

The message socked me between the eyes. *This was for you, Shawn Jayroe! Look at what you've done! You've done things that were totally unimaginable. Things that were completely NOT Shawn Jayroe. You were praying for strength and received it one-thousand-fold!*

I stared back into the mirror in total amazement at the strength God had granted me during Richard's ordeal. I sought and found Him in earnest. I had been there for Richard, even after his passing, with God at my side. The entire experience had drawn me back to my savior and changed my life.

In my renewed Christianity, I devoured the Bible, then gobbled up one religious book after another. After I showed my

---

[9] Jeremiah 29:11–13.

mother "The Prayer of Jabez," she typed up the verse and taped a copy to each mirror in my house.

It reads: 1 Chronicles 4:9, Jabez called on the God of Israel, saying, "Oh that you would bless me indeed, and enlarge my territory, that your hand would be with me and that you would keep me from evil, that I may not cause pain."

The prayer became my mantra. I read it daily and blessings flowed abundantly. Even with the loss of Richard at the salon, my profit remained the same with just the two of us as it had been with the three of us. But I still needed an assistant to help manage the shop and handle the volume. For some reason that I still can't explain, I filled the position with pure intuition when I offered it to a complete stranger who happened to be in the shop waiting for her friend.

There was something that drew me to her, although I couldn't pinpoint it. Within a few minutes of her arrival, I approached Denita.

"Do you need a job?" I asked completely out of the blue.

She gave me a bewildered expression. "Yes!" she said.

"You're hired. Start next Tuesday," I told her. The force driving my rash decision was so intense that I figured I could train Denita to be the assistant I needed.

Normally every hiring decision was a struggle. I never made such an impulsive choice before or since. I had a clear and distinct feeling that God was driving this plan.

"It's strange, but I believe you were sent to me," I divulged to my new employee. It was a surreal experience unfolding between the two of us.

"No, I believe you were sent to *me!*" she replied.

Somehow God was aligning me with Denita to give us what we both needed. Sure enough, I once again outgrew my space at the salon and expanded even further. Finally, my staff had reached eighteen people and included a world-renowned permanent makeup artist.

With God at my side, nothing would stop me.

> *One of the most famous recorded examples of early horse advocacy occurred in 1866, when Henry Bergh publicly reprimanded a cart driver for whipping his horse. This led to the founding of the modern-day American Society for the Prevention of Cruelty to Animals (ASPCA), which laid the groundwork for other organizations compassionate to the plight of animals.*[10]

CHAPTER 8

I was on a roll professionally. Hair Perfections flourished beyond my imagination. I expanded to a more prominent location and rented three adjacent storefronts to get the space I needed. I started ordering popular lines of various retail products and they flew off the shelves. Clients poured in and stylists beat down my doors to work there. My dream to manage my own salon was realized to its fullest extent. I attributed my success to God and continued to pray and praise Him for all His blessings.

Even my father took note of my business success. "I'm proud of you," he told me. Those magical words were music to my soul.

Of course, Dad took credit for the drive and determination it had taken me to grow my salon. In hindsight, he was right. His example had illuminated my path. His career hadn't been without serious challenges and setbacks, but he bounced back each time he fell, providing a valuable roadmap for my journey.

My professional life was on fire, but my personal life had fallen flat. Mom was three hours away in West Palm Beach,

---

[10] State Line Tack. "The World of Horse Rescue." www.statelinetack.com/statelinetack-articles/the-world-of-horse-rescue/10075/ (accessed 8/22/15).

struggling with the challenges of Frank's degenerative illness. Meanwhile, my girls were approaching adulthood, but that didn't mean they couldn't use extra hugs and moral support from their grandma.

"Move in with us, Mom," I suggested. I could lighten her load and her presence would help the girls and me. Our home could accommodate her and Frank if I transformed the two-car garage into an apartment, which would also allow them privacy and independence.

With Mom's consent, I jumped on the renovation project. Before long, hammers and circular saws belted out a raucous symphony at the hands of the construction crew. Finally, a beautiful mother-in-law suite filled the once-hollow shell.

Mom and Frank had barely unpacked the boxes in their new apartment when I bumped into an old acquaintance. Ten years prior, the man had been selling his forty-acre ranch that he dangled in front of me. At the time, it was completely out of reach. Any way I tried to slice the numbers, I fell short of the bottom line. The disappointment of having to pass on the opportunity had nagged me through the years.

"Damn, I wish I could have bought that ranch you had," I told him. "It would have been so much cheaper than the way I'm doing things. I probably would have been able to afford it now."

Each horse I rescued cost me $500 or more per month to board while I nursed them to health and then found them a suitable home. The charges racked up quickly. With my own property, I could handle more horses and make a bigger impact for the same cash outlay.

"I still have it," he said. "I've been renting it for the last ten years, and the guy who lived there is in jail now."

My heart fluttered, but I dared not get my hopes up. After all, ten long years had passed and we were now smack dab in the middle of a housing boon. Real estate prices had skyrocketed.

"How much now?" I asked him.

"I'll give it to you for the same price I offered it before," he answered.

WHAT? I thought, utterly astounded. I couldn't fathom the unbelievable turn of events.

I gathered Mom and Frank and headed across town to check out our potential new home. Suburban Tampa was just beginning to stretch southeast toward Riverview. Housing developments were popping up among the expanse of cattle farms.

When we pulled up to the property, none of us were prepared for the ramshackle mess. All Mom could envision was leaving behind her beautiful, shiny new suite for a dilapidated pit situated in a junkyard. Cars, crumpled beer cans from the apparent parties, and heaped piles of assorted trash littered the grounds. The house was in such disrepair that gaping holes in the kitchen floor exposed the sandy foundation below.

Mom cried on the spot. "Please, no," she pleaded with me. "This is craziness."

"I have to do this, Mom," I told her. She begged me to reconsider, and based on her desperate reaction, I declined the bargain.

For the next ten days, all I could feel was the opportunity of a lifetime slipping through my fingers. I just could not walk away again.

"Mom, this is my life," I finally told her firmly. "I have to do this. Will you please just support me?"

Ashamed of her initial reaction, Mom jumped on board and since then has been my greatest cheerleader.

The "Man Sent from Heaven" waited until I sold my house, then I bought the ranch, a property that had been rising in value for many years, for literally pennies on the dollar. The bank required a letter from the seller stating that he was aware of the market value of his property and the enormous discrepancy between it and the price we had agreed upon.

Like vultures, several subdivision developers swooped in to snatch my land immediately after the purchase. The Monopoly money they offered was outrageous, but I had been led there for a purpose so I never seriously considered selling.

I couldn't believe the amazing fortune that had fallen squarely into my lap. How had a hairdresser, a single mother of two, gotten her hands on this incredible property? I firmly believe that God held on to the desires of my heart and when I returned to His fold, He answered my prayers. The ranch had been His blessing and I knew from that point forward that He would always guide and protect me.

Since my return to a faithful life, I had been reading the Bible and watching Christian television regularly. During one program segment, the preacher spoke of the "Prayer of Jabez." I opened the worn book on my nightstand to reflect on the old prayer once again.

It read, "Oh Lord, Bless me indeed, Give me land, Large tracts of land, Keep me from evil, so I might not cause pain."

I nearly fell out of bed! I already knew I had been blessed, but this was confirmation reaching out to me from the familiar pages. I had unwittingly been praying for the ranch all along. My land is God's land and He will guide me to use it according to His will.

The constant roaming of wild horses wears the hoof surface to prevent overgrowth. The relatively sedentary captive horses don't move enough to control the growth of their hooves adequately, thus requiring trimming.

CHAPTER 9

My little piece of heaven looked more like hell. I pulled out four forty-yard dumpsters worth of trash, in addition to a bus and a boat. Burn pits containing glass and debris were scattered around the property. And that was just the outside. Inside was worse. Major construction was required to make the main living quarters, as well as the surrounding apartments, habitable.

Shortly after the purchase, I had a near-accident with my beloved Corvette in the unlit, rutted driveway. Its sleek low-profile design proved to be no match for the ranch. After I almost tore off the undercarriage, I decided the Vette had to go.

My prized baby would be swapped for a truck, of all things. I cried while making the exchange at the dealership. I knew it was just material "stuff," but turning over those keys hurt nonetheless.

The transition to our new lifestyle posed challenges for all of us except Dee Dee, who was now living on her own. However, my self-conscious teen, Breena, was at the stage of life that was all about appearances and looking hip to fit in. The know-it-all age when parents become the least cool people on the entire planet.

It turned out that living at the ranch was a nightmare, according to an embarrassed teenager. We had traded our upscale suburban oasis for a hellhole. We were rednecks, by her definition, and she banned her friends from visiting the house.

One morning I entered her bedroom while she got dressed for school.

"Breena, I've got a problem," I said.

"What?" she grumbled.

"The truck won't start so I'm going to take you to school on the tractor." I had no softer way to break the bad news.

She exploded. "Mom, please! No, Mom! *PLEASE!* I don't want to go to school! You can't do that to me!" She was desperate to prevent the greatest possible embarrassment of her life, but as she found out that day, you can't die of humiliation.

Breena and I both survived her teenage years, and later, when she finally invited her friends to our home, they asked her, "What were you so embarrassed about? This is so cool!" Teenagers!

While Breena had a difficult transition moving to the ranch, my greatest challenge was the enormous amount of work ahead of me. Thankfully, I had a good friend, Sandy, by my side. I met her, as I do so many others, through a friend of a friend at the salon.

Back in the day, Sandy was a cattle farm girl from Oklahoma who had hitched a ride to Florida with a friend who was relocating. At the time, Sandy was young and single, so she figured, why not?

She loved animals since childhood, especially the cows that she rode and named like pets. As an adult, she lacked experience with horses, but enjoyed hanging out with our mutual friend at the barn, which was where we originally met.

Now that I had a monumental project underway, Sandy jumped in to lend a hand. While contractors repaired the inside of the house, which included installing a kitchen floor to fix the gaping holes, Sandy and I dug in on the grounds.

Neither of us were spring chickens, but we are both built with the will and tenacity for hard work. She was a godsend during the early overwhelming days when she and I built fence enclosures. The existing six-stall barn and its paddock could house the horses I currently had, but I needed more immediately. With saws, cement, and lumber, the expansion began to take shape. We pieced together my future with each post.

The salon's grapevine is a powerful means to get any message into more hands and it worked to my advantage. News of my formal expansion into horse rescue was broadcast to the community and the phone started ringing. I realized immediately that the need would outstrip my capacity, so I had to be particular about which horses I'd help.

The answer seemed logical: the underdog. My mission would be to save the worst of the worst before it was too late. I wouldn't be just a drop-off place for people who no longer wanted their horses; I already knew there were going to be plenty of those. It wouldn't matter what breed, how old they were, or how much money they're worth. If I were to judge them on a scale of one to ten, I would take those that ranked as ones. I would be their final hope.

From the very conception, it was never only about saving a horse. It was about rescuing horses from tragic conditions, whether or not they could survive. If there's a fight in their eye, I will fight with them. If not, we are a hospice for their remaining days, as we were for a horse named Marigold. I knew the poor girl would have to be euthanized when we rescued her, but I wanted to show her that not all people are evil. Maybe I couldn't save them all, but I could end the suffering of each one who came into my care, one way or another.

Charity's arrival christened the official launch and forever established the rescued horses as the conscience of my organization. At twenty-plus years old and with debilitating injuries, the gray mare was a lost cause by most accounts. Beaten with a baseball bat, she was partially blind in one eye, her skull was cracked, and her front right knee was busted, making it impossible and excruciating to walk. We supported her feet with padded, protective diapers to make her more comfortable. Her treatment racked up frequent vet bills, and her feet were a costly mess.

Horse hooves are somewhat like the equivalent of human toe nails, and they require routine trimming. If hooves are properly cared for, shoes are generally not needed. A farrier specializes in these hoof-care services and our girl, Charity, met our farrier regularly at $200 a pop.

The money I had been spending to board the horses was now diverted into the ranch, and I had to work my butt off to stay afloat. Calls came about horses in need. I now had the land to handle more, but I needed help. Sandy and I could only do so much, especially when my hands were already full at the salon. More hands would be needed to tend to the horses, and donations would allow me to build more stalls and paddocks. I was short on people and money. The purchase of the property had only been the beginning.

Having heard by word of mouth, people started coming to help. I was pleased with the traction I felt taking hold, but if I wanted to play in the big leagues, I needed to get my act together. Formalizing the rescue as a nonprofit organization with 501(c)(3) status would allow donors to write off their contributions, making donations more likely. In addition, the designation would allow us to offer community service hours to student volunteers.

With the formalization of the organization, I needed an official board of directors. I decided immediately that the board would be small and the members would be in agreement with my philosophies. I didn't want too many votes over each decision, especially when the choices to be made would be highly emotional. The board would vote on which horses we took in and which requests we'd refuse, a process that had the potential to illicit soap opera–style drama.

Even more heart-wrenching would be deciding when to humanely end a life of suffering. As difficult as those times would be, I didn't want hassle and chaotic disagreement to enter the equation when it came to making the tough calls.

As predicted, euthanasia became a stumbling point with those volunteers who disagreed with my philosophy. The board, though, was comprised of members who were like-minded on the topic. I stand firm and unapologetic on my belief of not letting a horse suffer, even though some people disagree.

One example of staunch opposition stemmed over the case of Val. The forty-year-old mare far surpassed the twenty-five to thirty-year normal life expectancy for a captive horse. She seemed to develop some sort of dementia and began walking into things and falling, thereby hurting herself.

Some people said that I should wait until Val died naturally, but I couldn't let her keep injuring herself or allow for her to possibly fall and hurt someone else. I lost a dedicated volunteer over the decision to end Val's life, but the experience underscored the importance of having a small group of decision-makers.

My board consists of myself, as founder and CEO, Sandy as vice president and ranch operations officer, a treasurer, a medical director, and a secretary—all roles that have revolved in membership over the years. My board members and other niche roles, such as for marketing and fund-raising, have all been filled as I observed the strengths of volunteers and nabbed them for their expertise.

With my organization defined, I applied for my 501(c)(3) and flubbed the first application. Using legal help on the second try, we properly identified the rescue as a separate entity from the regular horse boarding, and RVR Horse Rescue Inc. successfully attained the golden status.

A simple three-letter designation seemed most fitting for a ranch name. RVR was both logical and memorable—an abbreviation for River View Ranch. I designed my first logo as ЯVR, which later evolved into a more sophisticated symbol of two kissing horse heads, shaped as a heart.

I was nervous and excited, but I was all in.

The bones of the tail are attached directly to the sacrum of the horse's spine [. . .] and acts to balance the input that is going into the horse's brain.11 Therefore, an unsteady horse can be stabilized by holding the tail.

CHAPTER 10

Our boy, Stormy, was on his last legs when we brought him to RVR and I was uncertain as to whether he could survive or not. Once we decided to try to save him, we prepared a stall with a thick, fluffy bed of shavings to cushion his bony body.

However, when we returned to our new member, he was too weak to stand, so we placed a temporary fence around him until he could make it into the barn. In the meantime, he would be safe and comfortable right where he had landed after falling down upon his arrival.

My Rescue Angels gave Stormy a hero's welcome. They took turns lying on the ground with him, showering him with love, and promising him he was safe. And, of course, tears poured out over the terrible condition of their new friend.

I waited until the middle of the night before joining Stormy in his makeshift pen. Medication allowed him to rest peacefully. I tried to soothe him further with my presence and quiet whispers while he sniffed my hands. If only the river of tears I cried could have washed away Stormy's horrible history.

The next morning, our boy had the strength to stand. We groomed him, redressed his wounds, and then inched our way to his new stall.

---

[11] Holistic Horse. "The Tail Is More Than Just a Fly Swatter." http://holistichorse.com/equine-therapy/the-tail-is-more-than-just-a-fly-swatter/ (accessed 8/22/15).

Based on his assessment, the vet planned to fuse Stormy's joints as soon as his rope burns healed. He would be crippled but able to walk.

After we realized the extent of Stormy's abuse, we took the vet's suggestion and initiated a criminal investigation. I was passionate about bringing him justice and vented on our Facebook page: "I have been on the phone all day . . . literally, no one is interested in helping us bring the bastards who did this to Stormy to justice. . . . We are the voice of these precious animals . . . hear me LOUD and CLEAR . . . YOU WILL NOT GET AWAY WITH THIS!!!"

Each day his new team of caregivers would help Stormy to his feet, scrub and wrap his rope burns and other wounds, medicate him as prescribed, apply ice packs, brush him, and lather him with love to compensate for what he had been missing for so long.

Stormy's treatment plan proved challenging. His legs needed to be wrapped for support, but the wounds needed to be dried out to heal—each issue was working against the other. Additionally, the antibiotics the vet prescribed couldn't control the raging infection.

Even with all our efforts, Stormy began slipping away. I would join him in his stall each evening to lie with him, feed him treats, brush and pet him, and will him with all my might to heal. Once he learned to anticipate my visits, his gray ears would perk in the direction of my arrival, even as he lay on his bed of shavings.

I took him for short walks during the day, balancing him by holding his tail. He liked to stop and enjoy the tastes and smells at the pond. Whenever I wondered if I was being selfish for trying so hard to save a horse that seemed unable to overcome insurmountable odds, Stormy would show a willingness to fight as if to tell me he wasn't ready to give up.

Each morning I wondered if this would be the day we would have to let Stormy go. All the love and prayers in the universe couldn't heal him, and his health continued to deteriorate. After another week, when he was moaning in pain as he laid in his stall, it was clearly his time. As difficult as the decision was, everyone who loved him knew we had to end his misery.

A steady stream of visitors came to say good-bye to our beloved boy who had become a sensation on our budding Facebook page. Social networking had quickly become our mouthpiece and revolutionized our reach into the community and beyond.

On September 30, we posted an update for his fans: "Stormy is close to the Rainbow Bridge, please pray for him and for us to have the strength. This has been hard and heartbreaking. Vet will come tomorrow . . . we will know his fate then. He is comfortable for now."

The next day the decision was finalized and we gave our followers another update: "Fortunately we also have the power to end Stormy's suffering . . . that is what we will do, with a heavy heart and many tears . . . we have fallen in love with this little guy, he deserves peace." Then later: "Stormy will be laid to rest this weekend . . . we are keeping him quiet and comfortable until the detectives get what they need for the investigation."

The vet would arrive at ten o'clock the following morning to walk Stormy into the afterlife. In preparation, Michelle and I arrived early to spend the final minutes alone with our boy. We lay next to him on the floor of his stall, talking to him, releasing tears of sorrow and anger, and saying good-bye.

Without warning, Stormy rose to his feet and bolted out the open stall door. He hobbled across the barnyard, putting as much distance between himself and us as possible. He was trying to get away, which both shocked and pleased me.

When the vet arrived and we explained what had happened, he delivered the good news. "This isn't happening today. He's not ready."

Our small group erupted in cheers and shed tears of relief and joy. The ailing gelding had just given his caregivers the motivation and willpower to always keep trying and never give up.

On October 3, 2010, our Facebook post read: "Stormy's not going anywhere yet, he seems to have caught a second chance in life . . . keep those prayers going. They seem to be working!"

As part of Stormy's recovery, a farrier made corrective shoes to help him stand more easily. By the time his infection finally resolved, it was too late to fuse his joints, as we originally hoped would be possible. Still, Stormy taught us a few things about survival and trust as he thrived and persevered.

Upon his arrival I had wondered how he would ever learn to have faith in humans again, but he proved that his capacity for trust was enormous. Whenever one of his caregivers or I came nearby, Stormy would give his full attention no matter what else he was doing and then limp over and greet us by sticking his nose in our faces.

He touched many hearts as he rallied to recover from the inexplicable torture he had endured. This underdog earned the distinction of being the only horse to have the run of the property and he was nicknamed Ranch Manager. He was always underfoot and in the way, but no one minded at all. Our Stormy had captured everyone's heart.

The withers is the highest part of a horse's back, lying at the base of the neck above the shoulders.

CHAPTER 11

When I first bought the ranch, an overwhelming to-do list loomed before me. One of the critical necessities was to establish medical care for the sick animals. Because I already owned horses, I was familiar with the veterinary services available in the area, but my new undertaking would require a different working relationship with a medical team.

I needed more of a business partnership than a normal doctor-patient relationship. My medical team had to be committed to supporting our cause, which often requires emergency response. Our rescues might arrive at any time of the day or night, typically with no notice. Each phone call was a potential emergency, so my medical team had to be willing to work on this often urgent basis.

It took me a few tries to find just the right match, but I did. Dr. Gold and his wife, Lisa, walked into my life during our "Hillbilly Hoe Down" fund-raising event and they quickly became critical members of the team. Dr. Gold's private veterinary practice is closely linked to Tampa Bay Downs racetrack. His work with trainers and owners runs him nonstop for twelve hours per day, seven months straight. But during the slower off-months, he donates his time to the rescue, supporting our routine medical needs at cost.[12]

Dr. Gold's mission to educate area equine owners on basic horse husbandry dovetails perfectly with our goals. He

---

[12] This donation only applies to the rescue and not the boarding facility.

performs wellness clinics, colic education (for the common and sometimes fatal digestive disorder), and wound and skin care lessons that all help to stem the tide of abuse.

Although Lisa has no formal medical training, her experience with horses exposed her to many illnesses and ailments. In addition to the knowledge she gained from owning two horses, she performed competitive show jumping from age nine to seventeen, at which point she began her career at the racetrack. As an added bonus, she has a direct line to the vet himself. Lisa became our medical liaison, the crucial link between health concerns at the ranch, which are handled by our volunteer vet techs, and professional veterinary care.

In conjunction with Dr. Gold and Lisa, the specialists at Brandon Equine Medical Center (formerly known as Surgi-Care Center for Horses) rounded out the superior and responsive medical team I needed. Brandon Equine Medical Center had existed for ten years before I opened RVR. Dr. Kuebelbeck was one of the two originating partners who chose to open their practice in Hillsborough County, one of Florida's largest horse populations. Their facility is the only one of its kind on Florida's west coast and it is centrally located in Brandon.

Their practice originated as a surgery center for horses, primarily for colic cases. The pristine state-of-the-art air-conditioned operating room might be mistaken for any human hospital facility.

They later expanded into a full-fledged clinic, adding outpatient services that include a full ambulatory fleet of doctors who work in the field. A specialized air-conditioned dental trailer allows them to treat patients in safety and comfort. The same trailer facilitates other on-site medical services, providing valuable "house calls." This innovative team continues to refine and improve the services needed for their growing clientele. Due to customer demand, the addition of a sports medicine facility is next on their docket.

Beyond their expert medical care, Dr. Kuebelbeck and her team have a genuine love of horses that permeates their business. When we put her compassion to the test with a rescue named Gracie, Dr. Kuebelbeck proved that our partnership with this caring and competent organization was invaluable.

Gracie's rescue began like so many others, with a call from a Good Samaritan whose "friend of friend" had a horse in dire need. The poor mare was being brutalized by a hormonal stallion that was continually mounting and biting her, as well as chasing her off her food. The scrawny girl was little more than a skeleton. Infected wounds ravaged her body. Watching the perpetrator torture Gracie was live entertainment for the despicable owner.

The caller pleaded with us to help the battered mare, as well as to remove the stallion so another horse would not fall victim to him again. In addition, we sought out another mild-mannered stallion that was also on the property. With some coaxing, otherwise known as threats to contact the sheriff, the owner relinquished the three horses, Gracie, Cowboy, and Rowdy.

Cowboy and Rowdy were both physically healthy but mentally unstable and out of control. We castrated them both upon their arrival, as per our standard protocol, and once they were sound and stable, both of the boys were adopted.

Gracie, on the other hand, was a shattered mess upon her arrival. Her withers was so saturated with infection that pus sloshed out of a four-inch black hole with each step she took. Her back and sides were shiny and sticky from the constant stream of goo. She was in such poor condition and so seriously wounded that I didn't think she'd make it. Determination in her eye told me she was a fighter, but her recovery would certainly be a long shot.

Gracie's back injury was typical for a horse that had been savaged or brutally bitten. A horse's spine is formed of a series of vertebrae that contain radiating protrusions of bone—similar to outstretched fingers—called dorsal spinal processes. The stallion had sheared off many of Gracie's dorsal spinal processes, most likely by biting her, and her condition was possibly exacerbated by continual mounting. The root of her raging infection was the broken and fractured bones in her back.

The bone fragments died without proper blood supply and her body then treated the dead bone as a foreign intruder. Inflammation is the body's natural mechanism for trying to push out an invader. Gracie's body reacted similarly to a human body reacting to an embedded splinter of wood. If left unchecked, the area around the splinter will begin to fester and pus until the splinter is removed. Based on the degree of Gracie's raging infection, her condition had existed for quite some time.

The only way to heal Gracie was to remove the fragments of bone. Our diligent team went to work flushing the enormous cavity in her back with Ag wash, an antibacterial sanitizer. Then we began the tedious work of searching for bone fragments inside the hole and removing as many as we could find. The crater was stuffed with mane hair by the violent stallion. Gracie's injury was beyond anything we had ever seen.

We tended to her wounds as best we could and she tolerated the treatments patiently—up to a point. Once she reached her limit, she began to fight us. *I'm sick of you guys poking and hurting me*, she tried to tell us through her orneriness, but we had to keep at it. We could see Gracie's improvement as we removed more and more pieces.

Our amazing volunteers provided phenomenal nursing care, handling Gracie's treatment like pros. The stench of the oozing vile slime would be enough to discourage most people from even approaching her, but our dedicated team stepped up to the challenge. Even the vets were impressed with the slinky-wrap our creative caregivers made to keep the wound covered between treatments.

Although Gracie's progress was significant, there was only so much we could do to poke around in search of fragments. The antibiotics and continual flushing were not going to be enough to heal her. We had come to the end of our rope. I couldn't afford the surgery that would save her, and so Gracie would have to be put down.

In a last-ditch effort, Dr. Gold appealed to Dr. Kuebelbeck and she agreed to evaluate Gracie. She identified the draining tracts of infection, beginning at vertebrae T4, but she couldn't determine the extent of the damage. One thing was for certain: there was no hope if they couldn't remove the source of infection, which also included any bones that were fractured and still attached.

Dr. Kuebelbeck considered Gracie a good candidate for treatment because she was relatively healthy other than the infection. Her ailment was isolated to one section of her back and if they could resolve the source of the problem, Gracie would be alright. Besides, Dr. Kuebelbeck saw the same determination in her eye that I did and everything else about the spunky mare told the genuinely caring doctor that she wanted to live. Gracie was thin, but eating well and gaining weight. Dr. Kuebelbeck both surprised and pleased me when she agreed to help our girl.

Due to Gracie's compromised and frail condition, her surgery would be performed under less-aggressive local anesthesia. With this method, Gracie would remain standing during the operation, but she'd be supported in an upright position using a medical stock. Although it's a high-tech system, the metal frame with slings and pulleys is situated in the center aisle of the open-air barn, beyond the comfort of air conditioning. The surgical team dug for bone fragments for nearly six grueling hours, pouring sweat in the oppressive Florida heat and gagging on the putrid, rotten gunk.

This process had to be repeated several times before Gracie's drainage stopped, which was the only sure sign that she had finally healed. Although the extent of the treatment and surgeries far exceeded what Dr. Kuebelbeck first thought and hoped would be required, she didn't regret her choice to help. She and her team remained grateful that their expertise had saved Gracie's life.

Once her surgical treatments began, Gracie's combative shell began to soften. She knew we were helping her and thus began fully cooperating both with her RVR caregivers and the Brandon Equine staff.

One ranch volunteer who doctored Gracie's wounds daily fell in love and adopted the recovering mare. However, it was a short-lived happily-ever-after ending. When the new mom realized her girl couldn't be ridden, she disappeared, dropping poor Gracie like a hot potato.

I couldn't understand why she thought she could ride a horse who had suffered broken bones in her back. It saddened me that love could be so fickle, but maybe it hadn't been love in the first place.

> *Most horses won't show the extremes of their*
> *personality traits unless they're under stress.*
> *Take them out of their element, for example,*
> *and fearful horses may become much more*
> *easily spooked and flighty, challenging horses*
> *may become bossier, and aloof horses may*
> *"just check out."[13]*

CHAPTER 12

As our volunteer base grew, we attracted people from all walks of life. Each one has had something valuable to contribute—their life experiences shaped what they have to offer. Sweet and quiet Cassidy kept to herself while she felt out the lay of the land. As she became more comfortable, she opened up about the road that had led her to us.

The twenty-four-year-old Connecticut native had no reason to suspect the swollen lymph node in her neck stemmed from anything but a cold or flu. After all, she felt fine and was in the prime of her life. How could it be more serious than a cold? But the bug she was expecting never came, and her lymph node didn't shrink back to normal.

A battery of tests detected a mass, yet none could pinpoint what it was. Even the specialists she consulted were uncertain. The doctors suspected it was benign, but the evil invader had encased her crucial carotid artery, forcing a critical and tricky surgery. She might bleed to death, they warned her, but even that terrifying possibility didn't override her desperation for surgery. It couldn't happen fast enough.

---

[13] Equisearch. "Know Your Horse, Know Yourself." September 1, 2008. www.equisearch.com/article/know-your-horse-know-your-self (accessed 8/22/15)

After the operation, her mind hung in a postsurgical fog when the doctor reported that the tissue they had just removed looked like thyroid tissue. It was being sent for further evaluation.

That's weird, Cassidy thought. *What would thyroid tissue be doing up there? . . . He didn't say it's cancer, so it must not be*, she told herself.

She was no stranger to thyroid problems, having dealt with the autoimmune disorder Hashimoto's thyroiditis since she was seventeen years old. Medication had kept everything under control so far.

A week after the surgery, the final testing to confirm the tumor's true identity was complete. The doctor shared the results in his office. The mass was, in fact, thyroid tissue. Cassidy hadn't been ready to absorb the words fully until the doctor hit her square in the forehead. "It's papillary carcinoma."

Carcinoma? she thought. *Wait a minute . . . that's cancer! Are you telling me I'm twenty-four years old and I have [bleeping] CANCER?*

A lame assurance from the doctor that thyroid cancer is one of the most treatable villains didn't soften the blow. The startling invasive Stage III diagnosis felt insurmountable. Not only did Cassidy have cancer, but it had begun spreading. The mass and lymph nodes had been removed in the initial surgery, followed by the thyroid a month later once the diagnosis was confirmed. Two long pink slices across her neck were daily reminders.

The remainder of Cassidy's treatment was a snap, a vacation of sorts. After ingesting radioactive iodine, she remained in isolation at her friends' lake cottage in Sturbridge, Massachusetts. The week of solitude triggered a major turning point for Cassidy. Meditation at the water's edge brought answers and serenity.

As anyone who has faced their own mortality can attest, the experience brings a new perspective and rearranges priorities. During her hiatus, Cassidy was freed from the pressure of lofty goals and ambitions and found true happiness just soaking up the sunshine and appreciating life in the moment.

The day following her release from isolation, Cassidy's girlfriend of six years proposed and she accepted. Cassidy and Doreen[14] were engaged to be married.

In the following months, Cassidy befriended Kara and Tara,[15] a couple who had recently been discharged from the service. The women would be attending college in Florida starting in the upcoming semester. In the meantime, they were working to make ends meet in Connecticut.

The two couples became close until the friendship sparked an attraction between Cassidy and the women. She soon fell head over heels. When a shocked and irate Doreen discovered the truth, Cassidy fled with Kara and Tara to their apartment.

In the coming days, Doreen begged Cassidy to come back. "We'll work it out," she pleaded until Cassidy finally caved.

But when she returned, there was hell to pay. Doreen stole her car keys and held her hostage. She pushed Cassidy down the stairs and jacked her up against the wall, pummeling her with blows and insults.

Cassidy happened to be on the phone with her father during one such beating and she finally broke her long silence. She admitted to her dad for the first time that she had been Doreen's punching bag for the better part of six years. Cassidy had mastered hiding the evil truth and the bruises.

Her father insisted on calling the police even as Cassidy protested. She was terrified of the wrath she had been promised

---

[14] Name has been changed to protect privacy.
[15] Name has been changed to protect privacy.

if she ever called for help. This wasn't the first time she feared for her life, but this time it seemed most likely to happen.

The police arrived to diffuse the altercation and Cassidy grabbed a few belongings and returned to Kara and Tara's place. They had been the first friends she confided in about her abuse. Their love and compassion had been just what her battered soul needed and she gobbled it up. They told her she was beautiful and worthy of more than angry beatings. Who wouldn't fall for that?

Kara and Tara were moving to Tampa soon and invited Cassidy to join them. Their romantic relationship had since fizzled, but they remained friends, though an unspoken awkwardness hung in the air. Still, the women were extending a lifeline that Cassidy couldn't ignore.

The free spirit had always dreamt of leaving Connecticut—a subject that had fueled many arguments with Doreen—but Florida hadn't been a place she ever considered. However, she was stuck in a dead-end job and she was alone. When Cassidy and Doreen split, she hadn't wanted to force their joint friends to pick sides, so she walked away.

I'm starting over, she decided. She quit her job, packed up her car, and sold or ditched everything that she couldn't squeeze inside. She then drove the 1,300 miles to Tampa while her new roommates awaited her arrival.

Shedding her life and landing in the Sunshine State gave Cassidy an opportunity to explore the choices that had brought her to that point. How had she withstood a violent relationship for so many years? And *why* had she?

The domestic violence hadn't begun with a black eye or a knife to the throat. It generally doesn't. No rational person would stay if that were the case. It started small, like throwing something across the room or punching a wall.

Domestic violence is an insidious villain. Like a boa constrictor placing the first wrap around his prey, it might be mistaken for a loving hug. The following wraps gradually form a full coil that slowly tightens. The defenseless prey finally becomes aware of the danger as he nears his last breath.

In Cassidy's case, the early incidents were relatively benign and the good times in between were deliciously sweet, keeping her hooked. Cassidy tabled her dream of becoming a writer when Doreen disapproved of an occupation that she considered useless and a dead end. Cassidy gradually became a house slave, taking beatings if her cleaning didn't meet Doreen's expectations.

She had spent the better part of six years enduring physical and emotional abuse at the hands of a master manipulator to the point that she finally disassociated from the beatings. Her mind convinced her that it wasn't real and it wasn't happening to her.

She recognized her desperate loneliness, but couldn't see a way out. Doreen had regularly accused Cassidy of being a cheating whore, although she had done nothing to give Doreen suspicion. That is, until Cassidy began to feel something like real love from Kara and Tara.

Doreen's explosive anger stemmed from her childhood experiences and Cassidy had been determined to help fix her. "I'll go to therapy," Doreen would promise, and Cassidy believed her time and time again. What kind of a person would Cassidy be if she left Doreen when she was so troubled? How could Cassidy leave the person who had seen her through her cancer ordeal? She found every reason to stay.

However, once her secret was exposed to her family and new friends, Cassidy found the strength to keep her distance from Doreen. But her new life was tough and lonely. She finally scored a job as a liquor store cashier a month after arriving in her new city. Thoroughly destitute, she scrounged for spare change in the nooks and crannies of her car after her bank account dwindled to fifteen pennies. Her father was supportive emotionally and financially, but Cassidy still couldn't stay afloat.

She began attending poetry readings in the evenings to share her heartfelt writing. But other than that one shred of happiness, Cassidy sunk to a new low, drinking her nights away. Her life was still a wreck, just in a new and different way than it had been.

She confided in her dad that she'd made a horrible mistake and needed to return to Connecticut, but he would hear nothing of it.

"You can do this, Cassidy," he told her. "This is what you need. You'll be fine. If you need to come back to Connecticut, I'll help you, but give it some time. Don't give up." His words gave her the strength to keep fighting.

Cassidy wasn't familiar with the shopping giant HSN when she saw their employment ad in search of advertising copywriters. She was deathly sick with strep throat and a fever of 102 degrees when she tossed her résumé to them without even a formal cover letter. "I'm an awesome writer. You should hire me," she told them.

With no health insurance and no money to get the medical help she needed, she was still running a high fever when HSN called. Thankfully they consented to a phone interview and Cassidy landed the job of her dreams. She was actually going to be a paid writer, something she'd been told repeatedly she could never attain.

Now that she had decent income, one major problem was solved, but Cassidy was still a lost soul with too much free time on her hands. In Connecticut, her life had been a chaotic soap opera, but in this new town, she had no friends other than her roommates, no family, and nowhere to be. She needed to start building a life. Drinking all night couldn't be the long-term solution.

Cassidy had grown up on a farm and had a horse as a girl. It had been ten long years since those carefree days and going back to her roots appealed to the spunky woman who had just uprooted her entire life.

She first considered riding lessons, but then decided that maybe she could do more. RVR Horse Rescue popped up on her Google search of "horse rescues" and Cassidy shot off a quick email before she could change her mind.

In no time at all, Cassidy became a regular at RVR. She forced herself to volunteer every Sunday morning starting at nine o'clock, a self-imposed schedule that required her to curb her escalating Saturday-night partying.

She loved volunteering but missed having a relationship with a horse the way she'd had as a child. *What the heck*, she thought. *If I don't spend my money on a horse who needs it, I'm just going to spend it on stupid stuff anyway.*

She was in.

RVR sponsorships put a dent in the care and feed costs for each horse, and one of our goals is to secure a sponsor for each horse we care for. . . . We welcome our horse sponsors to come out and spend time with their sponsored horse.[16]

CHAPTER 13

Cassidy decided that our sponsorship program offered her a perfect opportunity to develop the relationship she craved. While a horse is being rehabilitated, sponsors take financial responsibility that allows them to spend one-on-one time with the horse. It's like horse ownership without the piece of paper saying so, and it was a perfect solution for Cassidy, who was seeking something more.

Cassidy scoped out her options among the pastures of available rescues. Her initial attraction was toward one horse who approached her with interest, which is the criterion most people use when choosing a pet. However, when she spotted Gracie across the field, displaying not a single lick of interest, Cassidy flipped her logic upside down.

That one needs love the most, she told herself, referring to the aloof Gracie. *Challenge accepted!*

Cassidy has always been drawn to the underdog, such as the cowering puppy huddled in the corner rather than the rambunctious playful fur ball. She hones in on the one needing the most help, a behavior reminiscent of her choice to stay with broken Doreen.

---

[16] RVR Horse Rescue. "Sponsor a Horse." http://rvrhorserescue.org/sponsorship/ (accessed 8/22/15).

Cassidy knew little of Gracie's story, but decided on the spot that she'd sponsor her. As their bond began to develop in the following weeks, Cassidy reminded herself that a potential adoptive owner could snatch Gracie away from her at any moment, since adoption trumps sponsorship. A "Sponsor to Adopt" agreement strengthens the commitment to sponsor the horse during rehabilitation, along with the added plan to adopt once the rehabilitation is complete.

She loved the progress she was making with Gracie and hated the thought of losing her, so she began bouncing around the crazy notion to adopt the sorrel mare. *The last thing I need to do is adopt a horse. . . . My whole life is a jumbled mess. . . . I don't need a horse . . .* She rattled off her dilemma to her concerned but supportive mom.

Two months later, it was a foregone conclusion. Gracie and Cassidy belonged together and everyone knew it. Gracie's rehabilitation was complete and Cassidy arranged for the adoption to be finalized on February 14. The official "day of love" would symbolize their new life together. Gracie's adoption was Cassidy's commitment to her new life. No longer waiting for life to happen to her, Cassidy jumped into the driver's seat and chose her own path.

She finally had a writing career she loved, a beautiful horse to soothe her soul, and a growing circle of welcoming RVR friends and family. Any notions she had of abandoning her new life in Tampa vanished. She was staying for good.

After she'd already fallen in love with Gracie, Cassidy learned more about how her touchy mare came to live at RVR. She was amazed that their lives had mirrored each other's in so many ways. After suffering abuse, they had both surrounded themselves with impenetrable armor to protect their fragile, soft souls. Yet Cassidy resolved to heal herself and break through to Gracie.

In her effort to reach her traumatized girl, Cassidy began to gain perspective on her own life and the struggles she'd undergone. During her hours of self-evaluation, she finally recognized the painful truth: she hadn't loved herself as much as she'd loved Doreen. With more self-love and self-respect, she would have walked out long before she had. This clear perspective emboldened Cassidy to break her silence against domestic violence and she jumped on any social media discussions she could find on the topic.

As Cassidy spent more time at RVR, she became overwhelmed by the unconditional love she witnessed, both for Gracie and all the other rescues who might have been written off by others. The fact that Gracie was even alive struck a chord with her. People had stood by Gracie through her horrific injuries, even though she was not rideable and could be a sassy stinker. We never gave up on her. Cassidy saw that Gracie deserved to be loved simply on the basis of her existence, and she recognized the parallel to her own life.

Cassidy was showering Gracie with love, but still not accepting any of it for herself. By the end of her relationship with Doreen, Cassidy felt broken beyond repair, convinced that no one could ever love or want her. Ultimately, she realized that the outside approval she had been craving wasn't as meaningful as loving herself, and she came to know that if Gracie deserved unconditional love, then so did she.

Gracie's example as a prey animal also spoke volumes to Cassidy. A prey animal must ensure his own survival from the predators intent on destroying him. This example from Mother Nature is a valuable lesson for people who are drawn into abusive situations. If people thought of their own survival first, like a horse does, they would be less willing to tolerate an abusive relationship. At long last, Cassidy was on the road to recovery.

As for Miss Gracie Mae Sassypants, as Cassidy calls her, she grazes and romps with Lola and Annie in a pasture near the back of the property just beyond the big barn. Rushing to greet her adoptive mom when Cassidy approaches is Gracie's way of showing love, but then she plays a silly game of hard to get. In their time together, Cassidy is slowly whittling away at Gracie's hard shell and she relishes the progress they've made. The once testy and grumpy Gracie, intent on protecting her damaged back, now trusts Cassidy to groom that sensitive area. Each day brings new progress.

Cassidy loves her equine baby no matter what. After all, unconditional love is one of the greatest gifts in life, and these two survivors are finally able to share it with each other.

CHAPTER 14

Cassidy and Gracie are survivors of enormous proportions. Sarge is also a survivor, but with less fanfare. However, the poor gelding has three strikes against him. Besides being old, he can't be ridden, and he has life-threatening melanoma and heart problems. Boom. Boom. Boom. Three reasons it was unlikely he would be adopted. At the ripe old age of twenty-eight, Sarge had been around the block many times.

His lip tattoo, the branding given to most Thoroughbreds, gave us insight into his life. The faded marking seemed to indicate Sarge's grandfather was legendary racer Secretariat. Keeping to the tradition of his royal bloodline, the gray gelding began a racing career that lasted until an injury forced him off the track two years later.

Sarge then found his way to the New Orleans Police Department as a mounted patrol horse, where he served a lengthy span of fifteen years. After his retirement from the police department, he was donated to a therapy center for children with disabilities.

Once Sarge retired from his third and final occupation, he was fortunate to fall into the hands of a woman who loved him dearly, but who ultimately became unable to care for him. She turned him over to a new owner, but was later horrified to find

---

[17] Ponybox. "Fascinating Facts about Thoroughbreds." June 17, 2003. www.ponybox.com/news_details.php?id=2620&title=Fascinating-Facts-About-Thoroughbreds (accessed 8/22/15).

that Sarge was confined in a small yard when he wasn't being used as entertainment for drunken parties. One raucous rider after another rode him through the wee hours of the morning.

The woman requested our help after convincing the owner to surrender him, and we jumped in the truck to get our newest boy. It didn't matter that it was eight o'clock at night and Sarge was four hours away. This was our call of duty. Sarge scrambled into the trailer and arrived at his new home at four o'clock in the morning.

As of that day, he became a permanent resident at RVR, thriving among the herd and lapping up a taste of the good life. With the three solid strikes against him, Sarge is unlikely to be adopted, but he now has a wonderful place to live out his final years.

When Stacy, a volunteer, first came to RVR, she treated Sarge with love and kindness, just as everyone does. She'd heard about RVR from an acquaintance and decided to check us out. Her deep love and compassion for animals drove her desire to help them, but her menagerie at home already consisted of two dogs, Dakota and Chopper; two cats, Lielo and Gizmo; and two umbrella cockatoos, Echo and Nikko. She avoided volunteering at small animal shelters because she knew she'd want to adopt them all and her track record seemed to prove it. But horses were a safe bet because she couldn't bring one home.

She came to RVR with her heart open to helping all the horses, but also with a guard up that would prevent an attachment to any of them. She promised herself to stay neutral.

Her experience with horses began during her childhood, after life dealt her an incredibly cruel blow with the death of her father. Stacy was just twelve years old when a tragic car accident stole him from her. Many preteens struggle at that age under normal circumstances and Stacy had this terrible loss on top of it. The daddy's girl in her was devastated and floundering.

She and her mother moved to Iowa for a short time, where they had family support to help them cope. Many of Stacy's new friends lived on farms and it was there that she experienced horses and riding for the first time. The beautiful blond peanut also landed a role in a television commercial for Iowa governor Terry Branstad, in which she performed on horseback. Her experience with the horses in Iowa helped her survive that dreadful time of her young life.

Stacy hadn't had another opportunity to interact with horses until adulthood, when she married John. Her new sister-in-law lived in Michigan where she had a horse ranch. One of the most enjoyable aspects of Stacy's visits there was the chance to spend time with the horses.

Her childhood ambition had been to become a veterinarian, but financial constraints crushed that dream. Instead, she began aimlessly job-hopping. She maintained a part-time role as vice president of her family's pool construction business, but she had many more hours to fill beyond what was needed there. Her résumé also included hairstylist, silk-screener, forklift driver, winemaker, real estate agent, and property preservation specialist for foreclosed homes.

None of her string of occupations ever made Stacy happy. She had tried plenty of different avenues, but that empty feeling tagged along no matter which way she turned. Worst of all was the serious mental toll her job as a property preservation specialist took on her. When the housing crash decimated the Florida real estate market, the flood of foreclosures triggered desperate acts by those facing homelessness. Too many times, pets became disposable garbage, leaving Stacy with nightmares about the horrible abuse and neglect she witnessed. She lost faith in humanity and sunk into a hopeless pit of despair.

Stacy's purpose in life had always been to help animals, but she'd never fulfilled that need with any path she took. Her lightbulb finally went off when she learned about RVR. It was time to make her dream come true.

As a newbie volunteer, Stacy cherished the interaction with the horses. While feeding or cleaning the stalls and pastures, she also gave a dose of TLC, which allowed her to meet all the equine residents.

But one particular grumpy old man kept grabbing her attention. She'd find her way back to his pasture after her chores were done and began giving him treats and showering him with extra love. Before she knew it, Sarge had stolen her heart.

Our "Barn Buddy" program is designed for dedicated and caring people like Stacy. Unlike a sponsor who makes a financial commitment, a Barn Buddy dedicates time. These special volunteers make a commitment of at least once per week to groom, walk, clean hooves, and care for their assigned horse. When we approached Stacy about her interest in becoming a Barn Buddy, she was thrilled. "Who would you like?" we asked her, although her choice was glaringly obvious. Of course, she picked Sarge.

Stacy and Sarge both enjoy the weekly grooming sessions. He stands obediently while she bathes or brushes him. If no one's within earshot, she belts out her favorite tunes while she spruces up her handsome guy. She's no Celine Dion, but Sarge doesn't care, he just soaks up the attention. He knows he'll be rewarded with the treats in her bag, but when he tires of waiting, the pushy giant will rummage with his muzzle to help himself.

Stacy hadn't planned on getting attached to any horse, but that was before she met Sarge. She's kept her promise not to adopt one, but that's only because she's not in a financial position to do it. If so, she would snatch up Sarge in a heartbeat. Instead, she added Lily, a stray kitten found at RVR, to her pack.

But Stacy's true love is Sarge. He dominates her thoughts, even sneaking into her dreams, where she grooms him, rubs him down, and spends quality time, just like she does in her waking hours.

When Stacy first came to RVR she was on hiatus from her career while deciding her next path. But after experiencing true joy working with the rescues, she's now committed to ensuring she doesn't waste precious hours of her life at a job she hates.

Her love for Sarge and RVR has gradually morphed her original one-day-per-week commitment into two, and then three days per week. The fact that she rushes to the ranch before all her laundry is folded or dishes are washed is a testament to how we have changed this neat freak's DNA. Now that Stacy's work at RVR is finally feeding the hunger that was starving her soul, John appreciates the smile that has returned to his wife's face after being absent for too many years.

Like all of us, Stacy's heart breaks to see the condition of the abused and emaciated animals upon their arrival at the ranch. But her trust in people was restored after seeing our loving and caring RVR Angels shelter the broken horses under their wings. We've proven to her that there are still good people in the world.

The Barn Buddy program has provided a horse who is unlikely to be adopted with the consistent love and attention that he deserves. Sarge and Stacy are only one example of many horses and humans who benefit from this program. They are bonded in a way that brings great pleasure and peace to both. The benefits of our innovative Barn Buddy program are immeasurable. It allows a person like Stacy, who can't afford a horse, to form a beautiful relationship that's tethered only by heartstrings.

Equine therapy, also known as horse therapy, utilizes horses to treat people with all kinds of mental and physical problems. It's been used in the United States for more than fifty years and its history goes back much further in Europe.[18]

CHAPTER 15

The backbone of RVR is the army of volunteers, like Stacy, who are critical to the daily operation. Care of approximately twenty-five rescues is a tireless 24/7 commitment. There's no such thing as taking the weekend off, a sick day, or a vacation. Daily food, water, and stall care wait for no one.

In addition to the physical activities they perform to keep us running, the volunteers shower our equine babies with priceless love and attention. Our volunteers are drawn to the ranch for various reasons. Sometimes the path is simply paved with a basic love of horses. Other times, the route here takes a fiery detour to hell and back, as Mary Jo can attest.

September 28, 2008 is a date etched permanently in MJ's memory. Her heart rattled out of her chest as she punched the three buttons on her phone, then placed it to her ear.

"Nine-one-one. What's your emergency?" the operator asked her.

"I need help," MJ admitted, both to herself and the operator. Within minutes, she was whisked away to the ER. The next morning the attending hospital physician confirmed for her what she already knew. She was dying.

---

[18] CBN News. "A Happy Place: The Healing Power of Horses." June 9, 2014. www.cbn.com/cbnnews/healthscience/2014/June/A-Happy-Place-The-Healing-Power-of-Horses/ (accessed 8/22/15).

"You frightened us," the doctor informed her. "We almost lost you."

MJ's life had fallen so deeply into a bottomless pit that she could no longer see the light of day. She just couldn't "do" life anymore—at least not the way she'd been doing it. Ten days in the hospital restored her body, and then MJ admitted herself into rehab to work on her mind. She was finally ready to tackle her demons.

MJ's alcoholism had crept up on her, slowly overtaking her free will through the years. Because she could still manage life, she lulled herself into a false sense of well-being. She masked her pain, suffering, and depression with booze.

Life threw MJ a series of curve balls that expedited her demise. Her husband split, throwing her into a tailspin. In response, MJ fled Florida to return to her native Wisconsin, with her precious elderly pets in tow. Molly and Smoke, black Labradors, and Roo, her cat, were stuffed in the U-Haul along with MJ and her belongings.

Having pets precluded MJ from staying with family members, so a Motel 6 became her home for two solid months while she searched for a job and a place to live. In the loneliness of her tiny bleak hotel room, MJ downed one drink after another. Surrounded by her furry babies and stacks of moving boxes, she wondered how she had ended up at this point in her life. Her strong spirit that led her cross-country on a wing and a prayer was beginning to break.

She'd been a functioning alcoholic for many years, but the additional stress and pressure were dulled with ever-increasing amounts of alcohol. She was on the fast track to self-destruction.

From an intellectual perspective, MJ realized her drinking was out of control, but she was powerless to stop it. Without a buzz, the pain overwhelmed her. From a spiritual perspective, she believed her drinking was the one last thing God wanted her to finally turn over to Him. Without alcohol holding her hostage, God could utilize her according to His plan. She had been raised Catholic and had great faith, but she fought off turning this burden over to God until that fateful day in September.

In-house rehab cultivated a very thin and fragile layer of footing under MJ. She could feel the promise of solid ground beginning to form beneath her. By the end of rehab, MJ was on a path to renewed health, but she was still steeped in internal turmoil. The road ahead would be treacherous, but she emerged from her program with a brand-spanking-new attitude. The discipline of attending AA meetings helped keep her on track even after her release back into the world.

What she still lacked was something productive to fill her drinking time, which was really *any* time since she was unemployed. One day, MJ saw an advertisement in the newspaper for Stepping Stone Farms, a horse farm near her uncle's home. She had always been passionate about horses, but opportunities to pursue this interest were few and far between for a city girl. Until now, that is. This was her chance.

The crisp and colorful October afternoon was a perfect backdrop for a drive. Upon her arrival at the farm, MJ met with Lia, the executive director. The tour drew her in immediately. The charm of the old barn, the children working among the horses, and the majestic beauties themselves made for a magical combination.

She snapped images that captured the quiet natural elegance and promised Lia she would return with the developed photographs, which she did several days later. The pictures were a good excuse to return.

During their conversation, MJ extended to Lia her services while she was unemployed. She offered to stick around for the day if Lia showed her what to do and this led to an immediate crash course. Lia jumped on the opportunity and immersed MJ into a world completely foreign from any she'd previously known. Within minutes, MJ was putting halters on the horses, hooking them up, and leading them into the paddock. Once Lia felt MJ knew the basics, she moved on to another part of the farm to continue a long list of chores and left MJ to turn out the remaining horses.

On her own after only thirty minutes, MJ was overwhelmed and intimidated by the massive size and power of the animals. What if she did something wrong while Lia was out of reach on the other side of the farm? What if she forgot something Lia had told her? She panicked, but then gathered herself with a deep breath and boldly stepped up to the challenge. With that, her courage followed, which brought incredible peace.

MJ basked in the moment. The air was fresh with a sting of manure hanging in the breeze. The serenity of the horses permeated the farm and enfolded MJ. The senses that she had dulled for years with Bacardi and Diet Coke sprung to life in the raw nature. MJ knew immediately that this was a place where she wanted to be.

As promised, MJ kept returning and became indispensable to Lia, whose hands were full planning the monumental undertaking of relocating and expanding the farm. Besides, simply withstanding the bitter Wisconsin winter was a feat in and of itself. With MJ by Lia's side, they became a dynamic team and MJ's contribution to the farm was the perfect prescription for her recovery.

As one day turned into the next, MJ befriended the horses, many of whom had been rescues. She started developing connections with her new equine friends, which boosted her self-esteem. Her original intimidation was replaced by respect, awe, and love. Soon MJ was second in command, taking charge when Lia left the facility.

Unbeknownst to MJ, the horses were renewing her battered spirit and bolstering her self-confidence in a miraculous rebirth. Her urge to drink diminished with each passing week. Although the rest of her life was still in shambles, MJ now had a shred of hope. She felt God leading her out of hell.

A connection she had made at the barn led to a full-time paid position working with girls from a group home in Milwaukee. She had also maintained her part-time job teaching at the Red Cross, her volunteer work at the farm, and the caretaking of her parents. Yet she found herself drawn to helping war veterans like her father, a WWII Navy vet. MJ understood the benefits that volunteer opportunities could provide to the veterans, who often feel disjointed from society and lack ways to contribute. She began volunteering at the county veteran services in Waukesha and envisioned recruiting their clients to help at the farm.

MJ operates at Mach speed and now she was back in her groove. She was connecting with the horses, the girls at the group home, and her new-found veteran friends. Life was gelling and MJ was stronger than ever, but she kept herself so occupied by working and helping others that she neglected her personal life.

Out of the blue, Facebook made a "People You May Know" suggestion for a long-lost colleague of MJ's. She and Rick had worked together as police officers in Lakeland, Florida, back in the day. Their social media pokes to each other led to a rekindled friendship, which quickly ignited into a whirlwind long-distance romance. MJ hadn't had time in her busy life for a relationship, nor had she been ready emotionally. Until now.

She'd recently lost her job when the group home downsized, but she was still teaching part-time at the Red Cross. Her mother was doing well, though her father had passed away. It was time for MJ to bump herself up on the priority list. Could she uproot her entire life again to return to Florida as she and

Rick had discussed? Her two brothers lived nearby and would continue to help their mom, so that was not a concern. Her major dilemma was leaving the life she had grown to love at Stepping Stone Farms.

She searched for guidance and found a particular Christian music song that kept popping up. The lyrics of "Revelation" by Third Day became her prayer for an answer; *Give me a revelation / Show me what to do / 'Cause I've been trying to find my way / I haven't got a clue / Tell me should I stay here / Or do I need to move / Give me a revelation / I've got nothing without you.* What was God's plan for her?

The hardest part of her relocation would be leaving Lia and the horses. *It's not good-bye*, she finally told herself. *I'll only be a flight away, and I'll come back for visits.*

She had her answer. The die was cast.

A job at the local Red Cross quickly materialized upon her move back to Florida, and MJ felt God's hand guiding the pieces into place. Her new life with Rick was everything she imagined and hoped it would be. Only the horses were missing.

Her experience at Stepping Stone Farms had literally saved her life and the horses had become ingrained in the fabric of her soul. She yearned for the interaction, and her dear friend Lia was determined to help her fill the void. We all struck gold when Lia discovered RVR Horse Rescue in an online search.

MJ came to check us out during our annual yard sale event under the guise of shopping the wares. Sandy and Allison poured out the warm welcome that flows so naturally here and MJ's Stepping Stone tee shirt provided an instant common ground for the horse lovers. MJ felt at home immediately and Allison cemented the deal by offering her a tour. Today MJ is a cherished RVR regular.

A rocky road led her to us and she's grateful for the journey. Unfortunately, it meant knocking on death's door to finally bring her to this place in life. MJ's positive outlook exudes in her enthusiasm and actions—not uncommon for people who have hit rock bottom and clawed their way back. Shedding the baggage from the useless crap she worried so much about has freed her. Being destitute brought new perspective. As long as she has what she needs for today, she knows tomorrow will take care of itself.

In many respects, MJ and I have a lot in common. Both of us have fought hard in life and wear our battle scars with pride. As Christian women, MJ and I have taken different spiritual paths, but we have our strong faith in God as a common thread. And, of course, we share the love of horses.

MJ is able to share her zest for life and love of horses equally with all the equine residents at RVR. Many times our volunteers will fall in love with one particular horse who stands out, and this results in an adoption. MJ is a perfect example of a woman who loves horses, but doesn't feel the need for ownership. Of course, she's developed a few soft spots, most notably for Sarge. At the time the old man drew her in, MJ didn't know Sarge's background as a mounted police horse, which mirrored MJ's own career as a police officer. Who knew that old Sarge would be such a ladies' man, drawing in both MJ and Stacy?

MJ gets as much from her interaction with the horses as she gives to them. Through this fellowship, she continues to feel renewed with each encounter. The horses at Stepping Stone had literally been a lifeline in her time of need. Now seven years sober, MJ's brought her healthier self to RVR to provide a lifeline to our horses in need. Her journey exemplifies the beautiful circle of God's healing and provides a testament to His miraculous power of renewal.

Starfish can survive out of water for five days.
Then, they die of dehydration.[19]

CHAPTER 16

Incredible people like Stacy and MJ are shining lights in the dark and gruesome world of horse rescue. These Angels fight alongside me, helping me accomplish my mission. I'm under no illusion that I can completely eradicate abuse and neglect, but just because I can't eliminate the problem doesn't mean I shouldn't try to make a difference. The story "The Star Thrower" summarizes my intention perfectly.

> One day an old man was walking down the beach just before dawn. In the distance he saw a young man picking up stranded starfish and throwing them back into the sea. As the old man approached the young man, he asked, "Why do you spend so much energy doing what seems to be a waste of time?" The young man explained that the stranded starfish would die if left in the morning sun. The old man exclaimed, "But there must be thousands of starfish. How can your efforts make any difference?" The young man looked down at the starfish in his hand and as he threw it to safety in the sea, he said, "It makes a difference to this one!"

---

[19]www.answers.com/Q/How_long_can_a_starfish_survive_out_of_water&altQ=How_long_can_starfish_live_out_of_water&isLookUp=1#Q=how%20long%20can%20starfish%20live%20out%20of%20water (accessed 8/24/2015).

Stormy was one of our starfish. Nearly a year after his rescue, he had come so far, but the injuries he'd sustained in his abusive history were substantial. He had fought hard for the progress he'd made yet each day seemed to still be a struggle. His pain was evident.

One morning, Stormy limped over to me and gave his characteristic "in your face" greeting. However, this time when he approached, he rested his head on my shoulder. I basked in his affection. *How sweet is that*? I thought. But as he continued to linger with his head on my shoulder, I was hit with a devastating reality. *He wants to go.* Stormy knew his time had come.

I was crushed. Even though I knew the answer in my heart, I conferred with the vet, who agreed. It was time to plan Stormy's passing. We set the date for a couple of days out, giving his loved ones an opportunity to say their final good-byes. People poured in around the clock and showered our boy with his favorite treats and all the love and affection that he had always deserved but had been so lacking in his previous life.

In addition to the agony of watching him lose his fight to survive, the criminal investigation had not provided any justice. Maybe the system had failed Stormy, but his case made me even more resolved to fight for the others.

The night before the scheduled euthanasia, we purchased the supplies for a ceremony. It would be a special event befitting a precious soul. Pure white blankets would provide a respectful resting place and flowers of the most vibrant colors possible were selected. It would be a beautiful gathering with Stormy's loved ones by his side.

That morning, we loaded the golf cart to transport the supplies to the field in the back of the property, but something wasn't sitting right with me. I had been crying and praying for strength and asking for a sign to let me know if I was making the right decision for Stormy.

We laid a tarp down under a shade tree and covered it with one of the white blankets. I wanted Stormy to be protected from the relentless scorching sun. My tears sprinkled onto the bed we prepared.

Suddenly a large green grasshopper jumped onto the middle of the blanket. I watched our uninvited guest and thought, *That lime green grasshopper is so pretty against the pure white blanket.* Then I shooed the grasshopper, but it wouldn't budge.

Someone in the group said, "Maybe it's a sign."

Maybe it *was* the sign I requested. I pulled out my iPhone and typed "spiritual meaning of a grasshopper." I read the search result aloud. "Grasshoppers can only jump forward . . . .not backward or sideways. So, when a grasshopper shows up he could be reaffirming to you that you are taking the right steps to move forward in your current situation. Or it could be that he is telling you to go ahead and move forward, getting past what is hindering you. This is why a grasshopper is the symbol of good luck all over the world. A grasshopper's ability to connect and understand sound vibrations is why he is also a symbol of your inner voice—he could be telling you to trust yours."

Our little entourage stood in amazement. The grasshopper was indeed my sign that I had made the right decision for Stormy, and it brought me great relief.

By now, it was one thirty and the vet was due to arrive in a half hour, so we made our way back to the barn. There were twenty or so loyal Stormy fans on hand for the event. We sat in the shade of an old oak tree while the clock ticked down the minutes.

At exactly two o'clock raindrops fell, although there wasn't a cloud in the sky and the sun continued to shine as brightly as it had been. A surreal aura fell upon the group and many in attendance felt the presence of God among us. After ten minutes, the rain stopped as suddenly as it had begun.

The vet had since arrived and I requested that Stormy be sedated and anesthetized before his euthanasia to ensure he fell asleep peacefully.

We made our way back into the field with Stormy in tow. As we approached our designated spot and the vet saw the blanket next to the tree, she said, "We can't do it there." She couldn't risk someone getting hurt if they got pinned between Stormy and the tree.

My dam broke. I didn't want Stormy subjected to the scorching sun in the middle of the field. Shade would provide a more peaceful and respectful resting place for him. Reluctantly, I conceded and we pulled the blanket and tarp out from under the tree as the vet requested.

As if on cue, a huge black cloud provided the shade I wanted. God was helping me give Stormy the passing I had planned.

The doctor began with the sedation and we eased Stormy gently to the ground, refusing to let him fall. The anesthesia ensured our boy would remain still enough that we could safely join him on the ground. There we gave him our final caresses, whispered sweet words of love, and kissed our precious baby good-bye.

When the vet injected the lethal dose, the black cloud above parted, allowing brilliant rays of sunbeams from heaven to stream down on Stormy. He closed his eyes for the last time, grew his angel wings, and galloped off into the heavens.

Through my grief, a great sense of peace washed over me at Stormy's passing. Our group remained on our knees, encircling his still body. We wrapped him in a white blanket, then lovingly decorated his body with the bright red, purple, fuschia, and yellow flowers. Red rose petals adorned his peaceful face. The vibrant flowers popped against Stormy's white body, blond mane, and the white blanket as their backdrop.

Precious Stormy had been dearly loved and would be painfully missed. His hoof prints were indelibly etched in the hearts of those who knew him. He was one starfish we had thrown back in the water, yet he still didn't survive.

The rate of serious injury per hour is estimated to be approximately the same for horseback riders as of that for motorcyclists.[20]

CHAPTER 17

When we lose one of our babies, it always breaks my heart. At those times, I draw strength from the positive aspects of this difficult work, and there are many. One particular blessing is the caring people who dedicate their time to helping the horses.

Many times people's heart strings draw them to us initially, but abundant compassion and good intentions don't equate to horse experience. When unseasoned handlers end up falling in love and adopting a horse, their inexperience can hamper the relationship with the animal. Any horse can become intolerant and impatient with improper handling, but such is the case especially for our rescues, who have all overcome major obstacles simply to survive. One thousand pounds of frustrated equine plus one novice owner equals potential for disaster.

I've witnessed several examples of sloppy horsemanship skills that disgruntle both horse and rider and put both at risk for injury. Poor, sweet Jack was one example of a thoroughly confused horse. His rider kept clicking him on, then holding him back—sending constant mixed signals. Jack wanted to comply, but had no idea what he was being asked to do, until he finally had enough. He took off, flying straight back to the barn and nearly clipping his rider off on the fence. I was actually shocked that the man stayed on.

---

[20] Riders4Helmets. "Statistics & Facts." www.riders4helmets.com/equestrians/ (accessed 8/22/15).

He approached me afterward and said, "I need lessons. I don't know what I'm doing."

"You're right!" I replied. "You are really confusing that horse."

Sufficient training of both the animal and human is required for a truly remarkable bond to form. A talented trainer is able to create the most harmonious connection possible between a horse and rider. Our Sergio is a superb example of one such expert.

Sergio's father is of Cuban descent but was raised in Puerto Rico, a land whose history is steeped in horsemanship. The family owned several horses, but Sergio's father and uncle shared one particular Paso Fino stallion, a spiteful, ornery bully. He'd bite and kick the brothers, but ultimately, these belligerent behaviors helped the boys hone their horsemanship and riding skills.

After immigrating to the United States, Sergio's uncle settled in Miami and ventured into competitive equine sports. Barrel and show jumping, team penning, and cutting became his specialties.

In the western riding sport of cutting, the horse and rider must separate one cow out of a herd of cattle and prevent it from reentering the fold. The horse will duck in and out to block the cow only with complete cooperation and superb agility.

Any horses that perform competitive sports are highly trained, and therefore, very expensive; the cost can sometimes run upward of $70,000. Sergio grew up in nearby central Florida and, by age five, was walking, trotting, and riding his uncle's specialized beauties.

When Sergio eventually began riding less-seasoned horses, he was shocked to experience the difference. The perfection he had tasted while riding his uncle's elite competitors had set Sergio's expectation of all horses. In his mind, every horse should act as cooperatively as the highly trained ones.

As a strong-willed second-grader, Sergio embarked into horse ownership. Although his parents were set against the idea, they caved at Sergio's insistence.

Father and son were horse shopping at one of the local ranches when Sergio spotted Spartacus, a mellow, jet-black gelding with a little white star on his forehead. Sergio melted at the resemblance between Spartacus and his famous childhood crush, Black Beauty. It was love at first sight.

Having won the boy over, Spartacus still needed the acceptance of Sergio's father, which he got for his mild-mannered disposition. The laid-back fellow would be suitable for a child. With son and father in agreement over their choice, Sergio officially became a horse owner.

However, when Sergio attempted to ride Spartacus the day after his delivery to the boarding facility, he found that a switch had been flipped. His sluggish couch potato of a horse had morphed overnight into a crazy lunatic intent on trying to kill both parent and child.

In hindsight, Sergio recognized the flaming red flags that his family ignored at the time they bought Spartacus. The ranch rules had required them to call two hours in advance if they wanted to see the horse. He had never been saddled in front of them—it had always taken place in the back barn. His black beauty had always been calm, and even lethargic, an attribute that had seemed appealing in a child's horse, but it had apparently been a drug-induced trance.

They were forbidden from witnessing Spartacus getting loaded onto the trailer for transport to his new home. When he arrived there, he was bleeding from his head, chest, legs, and backside.

"He wouldn't get into the trailer, but we got him in," the seller informed the appalled family. The cattle prods they had used to force Spartacus aboard were strewn in the back of the truck.

Other than color, there was no further resemblance between Black Beauty and Spartacus. Sergio's boy was awful and evil, a demeanor that was potentially the result of some equally horrific treatment in his past.

The dangerous Spartacus was reminiscent of Sergio's father's vengeful childhood horse. His father realized they'd been scammed, but wanted to hide the truth from his wife because they'd paid a pretty penny for the bad boy. When Sergio would arrive home after being beaten by his horse, his mother would ask, "How's Spartacus?"

Sergio would try to hide his limp as he walked past her. He would muster his most convincing lie. "He's perfect, Mom."

But the determined child never gave up. He spent hours in his stall just trying to put a bridle on Spartacus. If Sergio's friends wanted to go trail-riding, he'd plan a five-hour head start to be ready at the appointed time.

He was bitten, kicked, and bucked off countless times, but these hard knocks formed a solid foundation for his future work with horses. For example, he can now bridle even the most challenging animal. Those hours of trial and error, patience, and endless determination taught Sergio lessons impossible to learn by any other method. Spartacus taught him that he could anticipate disaster by reading the early cues from his horse. He could then thwart trouble by reacting proactively.

No one could truly understand the struggle Sergio endured to tame his wild beast. His friends would brag, "I'm in Boy Scouts, I learned how to tie a knot," while Sergio would think, *Really? I learned how to wrestle a horse.*

When Sergio was fifteen years old, his family continued their expansion into the horse world by buying six acres of land. At that point, they brought Spartacus home from his boarding ranch and, in response to Sergio's growing reputation in the community, the family's single horse multiplied to seven.

Over the years, Sergio's finesse with horses continued to develop and impress those who knew him. His hours of literal blood, sweat, and tears led to stunning expertise. He began providing favors for friends who were having behavioral challenges with their horses.

"Sergio, you can fix this," they would tell him.

His knack for horses earned him recognition in an ever-widening circle of fans. One day he encountered a family friend, Katherine,[21] and her daughter in the feed store. Both mother and daughter are proficient riders and Sergio was aware they had recently bought a new horse. The daughter's black eye and battered face implied she'd been on the losing side of a brawl.

"What happened?" Sergio asked them.

Their new horse was the culprit. He couldn't be ridden. The cantankerous gelding was striking each time they entered his stall.

Sergio's friend, who had accompanied him to the store, piped up. "I bet Sergio can ride him." She had thrown down the gauntlet.

Katherine retorted, "You don't know this horse. He's unrideable."

"Then you don't know Sergio," his friend challenged.

As flattered as he was by his friend's confidence, he silently berated her. *Please stop! I don't want that to happen to MY face!* But his attempt to send her a telepathic message failed.

---

[21] Name has been changed to protect privacy.

By the end of the conversation, Katherine had handed him a check for $500. She would drop off her horse, Sunny Delight,[22] to stay for one week at Sergio's boot camp.

Sunny Delight was a freak of nature. He was a warmblood, bred for equestrian sport, and crossed with a Thoroughbred—a running powerhouse. A horse's conformation, or structural makeup, determines what skills they will most easily master. Sunny D's body was built for agility. He could leap up in the air and buck a rider off with ease, if he so desired. He performed perfectly and aced boot camp.

As it turned out, Sergio and Katherine each had a talent the other desired, and so they agreed to exchange services. Katherine taught Sergio the proper rigid English riding posture while he trained Sunny Delight.

During their training period, the equine student performed beautifully for Sergio. The pair competed in many horse shows, even attaining excellence at Grand Prix, the highest level of show jumping.

After Sunny D's graduation, Katherine took the reins while Sergio observed. It wasn't pretty. Sergio was able to identify the disconnect causing Sunny Delight's reaction, but was unable to bring the two to a suitable working relationship. Katherine agreed to keep trying, hoping that the technique Sergio had been using would allow her to win over her boy.

Katherine took her gelding home but the next day had to call Sergio after being thrown to the ground. She couldn't get near the horse. Sergio rushed to the rescue. He mounted Sunny Delight, who reacted normally. Katherine mounted again and he threw her to the ground. Sergio gave him a lengthy workout to tire him, but the horse continued to dis his owner.

---

[22] Name has been changed to respect privacy.

Katherine tried unsuccessfully for a couple more days before she gave up. She paid Sergio $100 to take the horse that eventually became his best barrel horse, covering his costs with winnings.

The young man's reputation spread quickly via social media. Marcy[23] learned of him through Facebook and asked him to meet her at RVR. Her dream was to barrel race and she needed help. At this point, Sergio had never worked with strangers, neither people nor animals, so the emerging horse whisperer had reservations. "I'm not a trainer, so I don't know if I can help you," he told her honestly, but they agreed to meet.

Once he saw Marcy in action, Sergio quickly pinpointed the problem. Although she had years of experience, her previous horse had been an old dinosaur that tolerated anything Marcy dished out. As such, she never learned how to ride properly. Her new baby was unseasoned and energetic, and he wasn't cooperating to her insufficient techniques.

To Marcy's credit, she agreed to restart with the basics. Teacher and student worked together three times a week, beginning with Horse and Saddle 101. After they completed the textbook basics, Sergio began riding the horse, which served to train the newbie, while demonstrating proper technique for Marcy at the same time. Lastly, he showed Marcy the subtleties of competent riding. She took the instruction to heart and went on to barrel race competitively, as she had originally desired.

When Marcy first invited Sergio to help her at RVR, he was unaware that it was a horse rescue ranch. He also didn't notice me nestled on the porch and observing his interaction with both Marcy and her horse. His techniques impressed me. The dashing young horseman had game.

---

[23] Name has been changed to protect privacy.

CHAPTER 18

Horse rescue has been a deep-rooted passion since the concept first crossed my mind. In the ten years since formally launching RVR Horse Rescue, we have remained true to the mission of helping the worst of the worst, with a few exceptions.

I'm accustomed to people tracking me down on the property. I never know what the topic will be when someone says they need to talk to me. Typically the conversation involves horses, but one day a man approached me with a request from left field. The thirty-one-year-old ran a shop specializing in rodeo apparel and he learned about me through the horse network. He was visiting from Georgia and had an unusual favor to ask.

Type 1 diabetes was destroying his organs. He was dying and desperate and wanted me to care for his dog while he underwent a kidney and pancreas transplant.

"I'm sorry, but no," I told him.

His dejected reaction yanked my heartstrings. "Why would you want me to do that? You don't even know me," I replied.

"Because I know you can love an animal and let it go when necessary. You'll love my dog, but give him back to me when I recover, or take care of him if I die," he reasoned.

Once I conceded, he made the several-hour trip to Georgia to retrieve Max, his beloved blue heeler. As he became more ill, the man lost his spot on the national transplant list due to his impaired autoimmune system. Diabetes cost him several fingers and he suffered a heart attack. His body was failing him in every way, but Max had a safe, loving home while his master fought for his life.

In healthier times, he has been able to visit Max. Other times, a picture would suffice. Max adapted to his new home and sticks to my side. Without cattle to herd, he patrols the yard and ensures my safety. He's the dog I never wanted, but when my heart told me to step up to help, I listened. It's what I do.

The other exception to our strict horse rescue rule was Hormel. The tiny, adorable, black-and-white and pink-nosed piglet wasn't dumped on us by an owner, instead he stumbled upon us and decided we were his family. While he meandered in and out of the paddock areas, he stole the hearts of the volunteers and developed friendships with the horses. By the time he ballooned into a 200-pound pig, he was convinced he was a horse because they'd been the only siblings he ever knew.

Although he wasn't aggressive, his size and presence began scaring our scaredy cats. For rescue horses who might be especially prone to spooking, Hormel wasn't an ideal pasture-mate. I knew the time was coming when we'd have to contain him in an enclosure. It was the only way to ensure his safety and protect the horses.

We all loved him, but no one loved him more than Karen. The big bully found himself a permanent spot in her heart when he inadvertently prevented another tragedy in her life.

Karen suffered a terrible loss when her mother passed on New Year's Eve, 2009. Six months later brought a devastating brain cancer diagnosis for her father, who died in October 2010. A final blow hit two months later with the death of her grandmother. Within the course of two short years—seemingly no longer than the blink of an eye—Karen's entire family was gone. Just like that.

The brunette beauty hailed from North Carolina, but her career took her to the Hard Rock in Biloxi, Mississippi, until

Hurricane Katrina wiped out the establishment. The company offered Karen a transfer to the Seminole Hard Rock Hotel and Casino in Tampa and she accepted.

The loss of her loved ones had triggered an assessment of her own life. What were her dreams and desires? What did she really want to do with her life? She pictured herself on her deathbed, thinking of what regrets she might have then, what opportunities she'd left unexplored. The answer was loud and clear: horses.

Karen's love of horses began at a young age. Instead of Barbie dolls, she played with toy horse statues. As an only child, "playing horses" was a favorite pastime she shared with her cousin. On one memorable visit to their grandmother's house, Karen's extended family arrived late in the evening from their home in Tennessee. The excited girls couldn't wait until morning to play with their horses, so they began clomping around on the wooden floors, making a ruckus that echoed into the basement. Their boisterous game of "horsie" was cut short by Karen's irate uncle, who stormed up the stairs and whipped the girls' backsides for waking the entire household at two o'clock in the morning.

The root of Karen's affinity to horses is hard to pinpoint, but her grandparents and other friends and family had horses that gave her an opportunity to interact with the gentle giants. Additionally, her father's love of the animal rubbed off on his girl. Some of her cherished childhood memories are of her father riding the family horse, Smokey, as well as his love of John Wayne and Mustang vehicles.

As an adult, Karen figured her own automotive Mustangs would be as close to horse ownership as she was likely to get. She assumed owning an animal required a large property, which she didn't have, and cost more than she could ever afford.

To fulfill her goal of "no regrets," Karen explored ways to be involved with horses. Through her research, she discovered the need for horse rescue, which Karen never realized was even a problem—a resounding sentiment from most of our volunteers. Once she began searching for horse rescues, Karen found RVR.

Shortly after she began volunteering, Karen fell in love with Diamond, a spirited and stubborn geriatric thirty-year-old with a bright white diamond stamped on her dark bay forehead. Karen relished the time spent with her soulmate and assumed the elderly Diamond would live out her final days at the ranch.

Fate threw her another punch when Diamond was later adopted by her original family. At that time, we learned she was actually only nine years old and not the senior citizen we had been told she was, which explained her spunky personality. Saddened by another loss, but not broken, resilient Karen continued to shower love on the remaining rescues.

In time, she found herself drawn to friendly, curious, and gentle Cimmaron, a giant version of a lovable puppy. Karen decided to enter into a sponsorship agreement. She would pay Cimm's expenses until he was adopted. Lo and behold, her original plan to not adopt got thrown out the window and she became Cimm's momma.

Her gelding loves people, but other than that, the 'fraidy cat is kind of a train wreck. Cimm's tortured past left deep scars in his memory. He spooks easily, even getting stuck under a trailer in one of his panic attacks. He's broken two lead ropes to escape being tied and nearly strangled himself in the process. In addition to his heavy emotional baggage, Cimm is plagued with a condition that causes his legs to lock or stick when he walks, an ailment called sticky stifles.

One evening the love bug was found lying down in the back pasture. We were concerned he may be colicking. His condition deteriorated and we became increasingly concerned, so we called Brandon Equine for a house call. The vet determined Cimm had swollen intestines and his body temperature kept dropping. She concluded the exam with a grim expression. "It doesn't look good. You have to make a decision," she told Karen, who crumbled once she heard the prognosis. The assumption was that Cimm's time had come.

"Oh no! Not on *my* watch," I informed them with a conviction I couldn't articulate. "I just don't feel it. This isn't going to happen today." I grabbed Cimm's lead rope and off we went. My aching feet and knees rebelled, but I jogged alongside Cimmaron, willing him to snap out of it. From out of nowhere, our pudgy Hormel chased after Cimm, terrifying the big sissy and launching him off on a tear. Once he settled down, Cimm was renewed. Something had clicked into place and the horse, who had just stood on the verge of euthanasia, had been given a new lease on life. Karen credits Hormel with saving her boy's life by nearly scaring him to death.

Karen came to RVR to satisfy her desire to work with horses, something she has received in spades. What she hadn't anticipated was that the caring and loving people here would become her new family.

CHAPTER 19

It warms my heart when Karen and many others tell me that RVR has become their home away from home and that our warm and welcoming people have become family. The inviting atmosphere is a precious by-product of the work we do, and it is further enhanced when family members join us as a unit.

Lindi, a young teen,[24] and her mother began volunteering within days of our intake of six horses from a barn of horrors. With no food or water within reach, the live horses were surrounded by the decaying carcasses of their brethren. The gang became known as the Six Pack: Phoenix, Britney, Goliath, Serenity, Cheyenne, and Boris.[25]

Lindi circulated among the sickly group, but was soon drawn to a chestnut draft mix gelding with a wide white blaze down his nose. Lindi plopped down with her chosen one, Boris, and there she stayed, firmly glued to his side, day after day.

Shy by nature, Lindi didn't interact with the other volunteers. Instead, she made a beeline to Boris when she arrived each day. There was never any question as to where she was. Wherever Boris was, the slender, curly-haired girl was certain to be, always with her hand gently resting on her new friend.

Lindi's love was instantaneous, intense, and obvious to anyone who observed the pair. The words that she couldn't express verbally, she poured out in a beautiful essay titled "Boris—My Best Friend."

She wrote, in part:

---

[24] Name has been changed to protect privacy.
[25] Name has been changed to protect privacy.

Riding a horse makes me feel like no other; enthusiastic, joyful, and energetic. But there is more to loving a horse than just riding it. Horses are brilliant creatures that become loving companions and best friends for life. My horse, Boris, is a rescued horse who [arrived] severely emaciated and stumbling. I cannot ride Boris, but we do have a forever lasting relationship that comes from true love and care, and to me, that is way more important than being able to ride him.

Lindi's devotion to Boris provided a magical example of unconditional love, even though her boy wasn't able to carry her. Her sentiment is one I wish more people would understand. Riding a horse is a fulfilling experience, but it isn't a necessary part of a loving relationship.

Unfortunately, in addition to being emaciated, Boris also had wobbles, a degenerative disease. He wasn't going to make it, and I watched him deteriorate until I knew his time to pass had arrived.

Normally, we gather a group to surround the dying horse with love and affection. But in Boris's case, I asked everyone to back away and give the whole experience over to Lindi. She knelt down and petted her friend until he passed away, while we waited at a distance. Once Boris was gone, we draped his lifeless head with a cloth. Lindi never moved from his side. She continued to rest her hand on his neck and gaze up to the heavens, as if frozen in time. My heart was torn watching this sweet girl in pigtails pour the broken pieces of her heart onto her Boris with each rushing teardrop.

The experience crushed Lindi and yet she and her mom continued to come to the ranch as often as before Boris's death.

Without Boris monopolizing her time, we had the opportunity to get to know the timid teen. Once we realized that her experience with Boris ignited an interest to help sick horses, Dr. Gold and his wife, Lisa took her under their wings and exposed her to some medical fundamentals that would help build a foundation for her future work with sick animals.

Another member of the Six Pack was Princess Britney, a Breeder's Cup nominee. When Britney's former owner found out the ex-racer had fallen into despicable conditions, she sent money monthly to defray our costs until the mare was adopted. Britney's adoption by Lindi and her mother helped soothe the pain of losing Boris.

Lindi wasn't the only one at a loss after Boris's passing, so was his fellow Six Pack buddy Goliath. Boris and Goliath had become best friends and often laid together at night. After Boris passed, Goliath slept by his lonesome self. One morning, during a wee-hour wellness check, we spotted our then-little piglet snuggled near Goliath. Sweet Hormel was doing his part to comfort his grieving brother.

From the moment Goliath arrived, the chestnut gelding with a bright white star marking on his forehead was on constant guard. The deep-rooted damage from his torture came, in part, by having his teeth knocked out. But our new volunteer, Barbara, was immediately drawn to him because he reminded her of a horse she had shown in hunter jumper competitions back in high school.

Barbara had experienced her own trauma with the loss of her husband to colon cancer the day after Christmas 2009. She spent the next couple years marking time, in no hurry to reenter the world. Her husband's best friend allowed her those two years to grieve before he started pushing her.

"You need something to do," he told her and followed up with a list of things she might consider. From the list, Barbara picked a folk-singing group that met once a month. After two months, her friend gave another nudge.

"Your singing group is great, but it's only one day a month! You need a focus." He followed that conversation with another list of activities to consider, this one included RVR, which piqued Barbara's interest since she'd always loved horses. She and her husband had bred American Paint horses, the beauties with distinctive splashes of white and dark coloring, until the recession in 1988 drove them under.

The idea of working with horses again had great appeal. Besides the fact that she loved them, they were too big to take home, making the horse ranch a better choice than a small animal shelter, where it was more likely she'd adopt a pet.

She came to check us out and quickly honed in on Goliath. Her goal was to befriend him, which was no easy feat. She talked to him from outside his stall to get him acclimated to her presence. When she reached in to pet him, he generally refused her affection.

Any contact with Goliath was a struggle. He needed to be tranquilized to care for his feet, and even at three times the required dosage, he still blew through the juice and panicked. It took everything we had to treat him.

But in October 2013 Barbara decided to take a small leap and sponsor Goliath. Unsure where it would lead, she remained cautiously hopeful that she could break through his armor.

Through constant dedication and endless effort, Goliath finally cooperated with the farrier and Barbara was eventually able to brush him. Although these are basic practices for most horses, it was monumental progress for Goliath. Barbara was pleased with her headway and adopted her big baby in March 2014.

She consulted a horse trainer, Caroline, for help. "He needs a lot of work," she said after her assessment, which came as no surprise to Barbara. The women agreed on a training plan whereby Goliath would spend two months under Caroline's tutelage. The outcome was nothing short of incredible.

"Are you sure that's the same horse?" everyone asked Barbara when Goliath returned to the ranch. The timid and skittish gelding had morphed into a more confident and curious Saddlebred.

"Yes, it is!" she'd reply, with her wide grin giving away her excitement.

Even with his significant strides, Goliath is still a work in progress. Out of all the horses I have rescued, he's the only one I thought we might have to put down because he was dangerous. Taking his pick of the freeze, fight, or flight instincts, Goliath would freeze, then fight. His fighting drive didn't stem from a mean spirit; the poor boy was just scared to death.

Barbara has traveled the path of healing alongside her boy. Friends and family were awed by her transformation into a completely different person. She has purpose and direction again. Her spirit is reborn and a sparkle lights up her eyes.

"We made a connection and saved each other," Barbara says and beams. Her story is one that contains a universal life lesson. Even in the worst cases, an extended hand and open heart is generally the ticket to a beautiful and lasting relationship.

Both the shape of the horse's back and the horse's movements make it ideal for [Multiple Sclerosis] therapy. Sitting on the horse can stretch hip joints and reduce pain and spasticity in leg muscles.[26]

CHAPTER 20

Florida, in general, and the Tampa area specifically, has historically been the off-season home to various circus families. Kit's childhood friend, Felicia, hailed from the Italian Cristiani Brothers circus family, famous for their jaw-dropping trick-riding horses act. The bareback equines lapped the arena as circus performers somersaulted from one running horse to another, jumped rope atop the running horses, leapt from the ground to a standing position on the running horses, and at times gathered up to eight people on two side-by-side gray beauties.

Kit's first visit to Felicia's house was based on the promise of riding elephants, but instead, Kit got hooked on their horses. Later, Felicia's grandfather, Daviso Cristiani, gave Kit Little Bit, her first pony. Having minimal experience and no money for lessons or other help, the fearless fireball trained Little Bit herself, using a trial-and-error method until she finally figured it out. Her experiences with the Cristiani family and Little Bit instilled a deep love of horses.

After her high school graduation, Kit spread her wings and flew out of town, never looking back. She attended college in Nashville, then built her career in the music and entertainment industry. One stint brought her to the heart of the Cherokee

---

[26] Multiple Sclerosis Foundation. "Therapeutic Horseback Riding Helps Rein in MS." www.msfocus.org/article-details.aspx?articleID=435 (accessed 8/22/15).

Nation in Tahlequah, Oklahoma, where she worked with the band Stealin' Horses. Back in Nashville, the little lady from Brandon, Florida, mixed with the famous Judd family, Minnie Pearl, and many other country acts and recording artists who called Nashville home.

One opportunity led to another and Kit found her way to the Big Apple. She settled into a 400-square-foot apartment that wasn't much larger than a Cracker Jack box, but Kit was thrilled to be flying up the ladder of success.

Life was a dream, except for one nagging thing. Strange health issues wreaked havoc on her daily life and as much as she tried to push the nameless symptoms aside, they kept creeping back. Finally, the doctor pinned an identity on the nameless thug.

MS.

Multiple. Sclerosis.

Shit.

With the diagnosis, Kit's previously confusing and vague symptoms now made perfect sense. The sky had been the limit for her charmed life, but now she was watching in horror as her dreams and aspirations vanished in a puff of smoke.

The physical indicators that the world can see, such as the wheelchair and the spasms, don't even begin to describe the internal turmoil that accompanies such a diagnosis. When your whole life blows apart like a house of cards in a windstorm, depression and anxiety replace any hope and excitement for the future. The added stress exacerbates the MS, and thus continues a vicious cycle.

With a full-on attack, Kit's mobility would plummet until she was wheelchair-bound. Thankfully, during healthier periods, her wheelchair sits empty and collects dust, yet it threatens to hold her hostage during the next bout. A service dog named Max Dolittle became her constant companion. His presence helped allay the anxiety and panic attacks that can be symptomatic of this ruthless diagnosis.

During one visit to Florida, Kit and her mom were invited to the home of a mounted police officer. The conversation turned to Kit's childhood love of horses and how their scent had always brought her peace. Whenever she was stressed or nervous, the smell of a sweaty horse would calm her. It had been a remarkable drug of choice.

After their conversation, the woman presented Kit with plastic baggies containing cloths she had moistened by wiping down two sweaty retired mounted police horses she owned. Kit returned to New York City with a dose of her favorite perfume and a bright idea.

Her brother lived near Central Park. From his place, Kit and Max made their way to the restaurant Tavern on the Green in search of the carriage horses waiting outside for potential fares to emerge. She was armed with fresh washcloths and baggies that would preserve her prize. The perplexed carriage drivers allowed Kit to take her sweaty samples and thus began Kit and Max's routine.

"I was a huffer," Kit says, joking about inhaling from her baggies, but she was serious. "Horse people understand that, but all my friends in New York just thought I was crazy," she recalls.

After fourteen years, her lightbulb finally went off. Kit was grateful for the opportunity to live in the city that never sleeps and her regular doses of "horse smell" were helping her cope. There were endless possibilities of things to do at any hour of the day or night. And yet where did she spend her time? She and Max sat at Tavern on the Green, while Kit petted the horses and collected their sweat. She could no longer deal with the constant stresses of living in such a frenzied environment, one that physically and mentally outpaced her.

She wanted to be with horses again. She needed it. Her search for horse rescues or other opportunities in NYC came up empty, as she'd expected, but the idea had been planted and started to take root in the back of her mind. As much as she loved the Big Apple, it was time to return to her southern roots, and the most logical option was Brandon, Florida.

Meanwhile, another setback was dumped on top of her MS struggles: A breast cancer diagnosis was treated with surgical lumpectomies for the first couple of spots. However, when another cancerous area was detected, Kit's doctor recommended bilateral radical mastectomy, meaning both breasts would be gone. She was devastated. *No. No way.* Between the MS and the continual lumpectomies, she was done. *I'm not doing that*, she decided.

Instead, she underwent another lumpectomy but also embarked on the holistic Gerson Therapy. This approach is a natural treatment that activates the body's extraordinary ability to heal itself through an organic, vegetarian diet, raw juices, coffee enemas, and natural supplements.[27] Kit chose a combination of traditional and alternative medicine while she continued regular breast screenings and subsequent lumpectomies.

God must have a reason for all of this, so I better try to figure it out, she finally told herself after settling back in the Sunshine State. Kit's friend, our medical liaison Lisa Gold, suggested she check us out, giving Kit a spark of hope for the first time in a very long time. Horses. Her magical medicine might be just around the corner.

Kit fired off an email inquiring about opportunities, but she was too excited to wait for a response. She drove over instead. Sandy and I were in the middle of feeding, so we welcomed Kit

---

[27] The Gerson Institute. http://gerson.org/gerpress/ (accessed 8/22/15).

to tag along on the golf cart with us while we showed her around and explained our mission.

Kit later told me that while she bumped along the dirt paths, seeing the pastures full of rescued babies and the good people helping them, she knew this was it. She was supposed to be here.

Kit's health was hanging by a very fragile thread, but shortly before she arrived at RVR, her body decided to cooperate again. She attributed a dramatic health improvement to both dietary changes and stress reduction. Her diet is now gluten-free and includes regular fasting. Her prescription for stress reduction is regular horse therapy, which happens by osmosis when she arrives at our gates.

The city life she left behind is a wonderful memory, but she wouldn't go back. She's found greater happiness being dirt poor and shoveling horse poop. Kit summarizes a common struggle for the physically challenged: "When you're disabled or have limitations that don't allow you to function at a level you once did, you have a tendency to feel disposable—not unlike the rescue horses."

Being at RVR has taught her that she's not disposable. The horses have given her an improved quality of life, and that's more valuable than all the money in the world.

> *The mother horse, or mare, is pregnant (or "in foal") for 11 months. Offspring are fully grown by 3 to 4 years of age.*[28]

CHAPTER 21

Shortly after Kit's arrival, we were asked to take in some horses in the aftermath of a police crackdown. The victims were being divvied up among various rescue sites.

This particular case in northern Florida involved thirteen horses who were imprisoned in a tiny, sweltering shed. Three of them died and the others stumbled among the decaying carcasses. The live horses had been impounded by the police and needed homes.

We often don't see abusers brought to justice, but this case ended with a conviction. The twenty-four-year-old perpetrator was charged with ten counts of animal cruelty and sentenced to jail time.

We had planned to take three of the victims, but one of the three, a pregnant mare, died before we even arrived to retrieve them. One of the remaining two we rescued was a baby named Bry. His mother was one of the fallen. The poor colt had watched his mommy die and rot in their prison.

Without a parent, Bry attached himself to a gelding named Jack, the other horse we took from the group. Barbed wire in the shed had somehow entangled Jack's penis. The sheath had enlarged like a bell, preventing proper retraction. A vet surmised that the damage was irreversible, however Kit later proved him wrong by treating him daily until the swelling was gone and his nerve damage was resolved.

---

[28] "Interesting Horse Facts." www.angelfire.com/tx2/horsecorral/facts.html (accessed 8/22/15).

After Jack's rehabilitation, he was adopted by a mother with young children and they moved Jack to another boarding facility. The normally content boy fell into such a depression with the change of surroundings that he eventually ended up back at RVR, where he perked up immediately upon seeing his Bry.

When Baby Bry first arrived, he was petrified of people. The vet had to rope him in order to get close enough to perform the required testing. We started leaving his halter on and lead rope attached, even while he was in his stall, because no one could catch him otherwise.

Kit was our newbie volunteer at the time and her interaction with the horses impressed me, so I thought I'd give her Bry as a project. "Why don't you go play with that little fella over there?" I suggested.

She would sit with him for endless hours in the stall, but fear still loomed large in the whites of the baby's eyes.

During the days they spent together, Kit fell under Bry's adorable spell. She nursed him with love and patience until she finally had a breakthrough and earned his trust. By that time, it was mutual love.

Kit's mom knew how hard her daughter had fallen for Bry, but still she joked that the little guy looked like a throwaway mule from a third-world country that no one else would want. Then she proceeded to adopt him as a birthday present for her daughter.

We planned a small gathering to celebrate Kit's birthday and her new ownership of Bry. Our original idea was to decorate Bry's halter and ceremoniously deliver him to his new mom during the party. However, Bry revolted and no one could catch the frightened bugger, let alone decorate or lead him.

Exasperated, I finally gave up. "Would you just go get your horse?" I asked Kit. It was the only way we would get Bry to the party. He made it clear that day that he still had a lot to learn about trusting humans.

Over time, Kit coaxed Bry out of his shell, and his personality bloomed larger than life. The coward blossomed into a goofy groomer. He licks the barn cats and cowbirds resting on the rails. And then there's Hormel. The bossy pig considers Bry his personal masseuse. During the days when Hormel ran freely on the property, he would enter the paddock, snort his request, and Bry would dutifully respond. Hormel would drop to the ground, lift his legs, turn, and roll into the necessary positions to ensure Bry reached all the right spots. It was hard to tell who enjoyed the experience more.

As Bry recovered emotionally and socially, Kit began working with him in the round pen. At first she would only sit on his back. Once he acclimated to that, she attempted to walk him forward, but he refused while she was mounted. He would back up with ease, but wouldn't budge forward.

One day Kit sat impatiently atop her boy who was still stuck in reverse. Meanwhile, Hormel meandered under the fence and started squealing to his buddy Bry. It was grooming time. Hormel dropped to his knees, then rolled onto his back, waiting for his session to begin. As always, Bry meandered over to his waiting customer, walking forward with human cargo on his back for the first time. It took a pig ten seconds to accomplish what Kit had been working on for an hour and a half, but she finally got her breakthrough.

Once Bry recovered from his prior trauma and began to trust and lead a normal horse life, Kit fell in love with her next basket case. Shadow was a mental train wreck. No one could get near him, but he drew Kit in like a magnet. His scars explained the torment he'd endured. Shadow gravitated toward Bry as his protector, even though Bry was a baby by comparison. The boys formed a friendship that evolved into a kinship Kit couldn't ignore. Now they're brothers. Both scream bloody murder when the one is removed from the other's presence. Their high-pitched little girly shrieks are a hysterical and endearing testament to their tight bond.

Other than her struggle to get Bry to walk forward, Kit is a natural with the horses. Her training in Reiki, the Japanese technique that uses touch to transfer energy for stress reduction and healing, gives her another method of connecting with the animals. Her sense of calm draws them to her.

After seeing her in action, I invited Kit to assist me on some rescues. In one case, she went to investigate a situation we had heard about, but each time we drove by, the horses were either specks in the distance or not visible. A very strong feeling that something was terribly wrong with the horses drew Kit to the property again, where she noticed turkey vultures circling above—a signal of imminent death below.

In the pasture, she saw two Arabian mares. Eve, as she was later to be named, was down in distress, while the other, later named Shanti, was standing near. When Kit approached the fence, a sweet and gentle Shanti greeted her from the inside.

Kit developed a quick connection before the desperate girl grabbed her by the belt through the fence and pulled, as if to say, "Come with me," which Kit did. Shanti led Kit to Eve, who lay dying on the ground, barely able to raise her head.

It was painfully apparent that Eve's condition was already beyond hope. The belligerent landowner refused to let us call a vet to euthanize her humanely, saying he would just shoot her in the head. As devastated as we were, we were powerless to stop it.

The Hillsborough County sheriff's detectives convinced the owner to allow us to remove Shanti, but we were forced to leave Eve behind. After the girls kissed their heart-wrenching final good-bye, Shanti scampered to the safety of our trailer, while her friend waited in the field to die alone.

CHAPTER 22

To an inexperienced bystander, poor Shanti and Eve may have appeared to be perfectly normal horses grazing in a field. A bleeding or lame animal is an obvious sign of trouble, but what about cases that aren't clear-cut? How does a person decide if help is warranted?

Many people are unsure what steps to take when they see a starving horse. From afar, one might not even notice how thin they were, and someone unfamiliar with horses may not know when skinny becomes too skinny.

Shanti and Eve's case was my final straw. An idea that had been ruminating for years finally gelled. We needed a program to educate the public. Good Samaritans are the eyes and ears within the community. They needed to know how to identify a horse in trouble and what to do if they saw one. After all, no one but us humans can protect the defenseless animals.

In order for our message to be effective, it needed to be crystal clear. And so was born our C.L.E.A.R initiative in May 2013. Care. Learn. Educate. Act. Rescue. C.L.E.A.R would be arms reaching out to educate the community. By banding together, we would become the voice for the voiceless and stop abuse and neglectful treatment of horses across the country.

My original idea involved placing ads in newspapers, urging citizens to take action if they saw an animal suffering.

Because horses are usually in remote pastures on lazy country roads, it's up to those few passersby who might notice something amiss to act.

The public needed to understand to what agency to report a concern. For example, Animal Services can't help because horses are under the sheriff's jurisdiction, at least in Florida. We documented the basic steps a concerned individual should take to properly collect evidence that will help law enforcement and animal control better protect horses.

Photos:

Do not trespass! Photos are a key piece of evidence in starting a cruelty case. If possible, use the camera's time and date stamp. Do not post photos on social media networks. This common mistake will jeopardize your case and the welfare of the animal by making it harder for law enforcement to do their job. People who see the photos may begin contacting and threatening the abuser, which might prompt him or her to move the animal to another location.

Know the law:

Laws regarding cruelty, abuse, and neglect vary from state to state. If you are unsure of these laws you can do a simple Google search or contact your local animal control or sheriff's department. Most sheriff's departments have agricultural units that specialize in horses and other livestock. It is critical to stay calm and keep professional when contacting authorities. If you aren't getting a satisfactory response from law enforcement, start at the bottom and work your way up the chain of command. For any conversation, always have your documented facts on hand.

Documented facts:

Documentation is one of the most important things for the animal and your case, so document, document, document! Document any incidents you have witnessed, including time and date. Take notes on conversations with law enforcement officials, including names, badge numbers, date, and time.

Don't give up on those who need an advocate. Determination and persistence pay off, but emotional or irrational behavior will get you nowhere. Professionalism achieves results.[29]

. . .

Now that we'd formally launched an educational arm, I needed someone to drive the effort. Historically, whenever I have a need, the right person always seems to accept the challenge. In this case, it was Angel Debbie.

Debbie M. had been hesitant to join her son to watch the movie *War Horse* because she assumed it wouldn't end well for the animal. However, she relented after his pleading. Somewhere in those action-packed two hours, an old longing tugged at her heartstrings. As they exited the theater, she told her boy, "I miss being around horses."

Debbie M. had taken riding lessons as an adult in New Hampshire. But since their move to Florida, that luxury wasn't in the budget. She hadn't given much thought to horses until the movie resurrected her cherished memories. The following morning an article about RVR jumped out from the newspaper and Debbie M. knew she needed to call.

Once she began volunteering, the horses filled the void that had recently stung her. Debbie M. showered love on all the

---

[29] RVR Horse Rescue's Facebook page.
www.facebook.com/RVRHorseRescue (accessed 8/22/15). page

residents, but was drawn to the unadoptables, specifically Chancey, an OTTB mare, meaning "off the track" Thoroughbred, or ex-racer.

Chancey's pasture is affectionately known by the older volunteers as the "Sassy Seniors" and by the youngsters as the "Geriatrics." Although not all are elderly, some of the residents, like Chancey, are simply buried in their past trauma. Her attachment to her stall and the paddock makes her unlikely to be adopted, which led Debbie M. and fellow volunteer Debbie P. to share the cost of long-term sponsorship of the girl they both love. Splitting the cost made it more affordable and allowed both women the privilege of one-on-one time with Chancey.

During their private time, Debbie M. attempts to penetrate the fortress surrounding the broken mare. A simple walk around the property, which should be an enjoyable adventure, leaves Chancey panting and panicking by the time they approach the front gate. Debbie M. celebrates the milestone of reaching the road with plenty of body rubs, praise, and carrots—anything to make being out of her element a positive experience for the troubled girl.

Chancey's health challenges are another strike against a potential adoption. Injuries from being ridden beyond her limits led to arthritis, a weak back, and leg ailments. The sweet and gentle soul is the nurturer of her herd, making her the low mare on the totem pole, and therefore, the target of bullying from her pasture mates. To stop the unfriendly encounters, we moved Chancey into the adjacent enclosure, where she threw a raging temper tantrum even though her old roommates were in plain sight through the fence. We answered her pleas and opened the gate, careful not to be trampled by the brown flash tearing back into her safe haven.

As part of Debbie M.'s training plan for Chancey, she volunteered to help host a local church group of thirty people, with one stipulation. Her nervous Nellie had to be one of the horses showcased. The experience would be a challenge for Chancey that would hopefully peel away a layer of armor. During the event, Chancey knocked it out of the park, allowing all the visitors to pet her. It was a breakthrough, and the children were oblivious that their tiny hands were healing the giant mare.

With the formalization of our C.L.E.A.R initiative, Debbie M. was the perfect spokeswoman. As an elementary school educator, Debbie M. also shared a passion for humane education and had already offered her services to me if the need arose.

With Debbie M.'s connections, we could make inroads at the schools and reach children, the leaders of tomorrow. By educating the next generation, we could stem the tide of ignorance and abuse to prevent the tragic outcome of poor souls like Shanti and Eve.

CHAPTER 23

Any program that involves children is valuable for our mission, and so Debbie M. began brainstorming ways to reach children within the community. In addition to the programs we would serve to the kids, Debbie M. also realized the value of incorporating children as teachers and spokespeople for our cause. One particular RVR teen seemed to fit the bill perfectly.

Young Alyssa learned about RVR through the grapevine at her school when she needed to perform community service hours. In addition to her high school curriculum, Alyssa took veterinary classes that culminated in a Vet Assistant certification during her senior year, an accomplishment that demonstrated her willingness to learn, impressive drive, and love of animals.

Her interest in horses hadn't waned even though her first experience as a young child was a terrible one. An unguided trail ride turned into a nightmare when the horse she was riding ran her into trees and tried to throw her off. Undeterred, Alyssa jumped right back into the saddle when her grandfather gave her riding lessons, which she continued for several years.

Because Alyssa was underage and couldn't volunteer on her own, her mom, Amanda, checked us out on Facebook before deciding we were a good match for their interests. Once they arrived, the mother-daughter duo quickly became staples, coming in one or two days a week. Their fate was sealed when they fell in love with and later adopted draft mix Thunder, a huge, stubborn alpha male.

RVR fits the ladies like a glove. Alyssa became so comfortable that she forgets she's here for the community service hours and sometimes neglects to log her time for the credit she is due.

When she established herself as a regular, people starting nabbing Alyssa for various activities. Allison, our volunteer coordinator, trained Alyssa to conduct orientations, so when Alyssa turns eighteen she will be qualified to perform them solo.

Along with volunteer Charity, Alyssa evolved into Debbie M.'s go-to girl for community outreach, such as family fun days, music festivals, and Dogtoberfest, to which they brought a minihorse. Participation in public events became a turning point for the young lady. It is at these events that her passion for RVR and C.L.E.A.R. overrides her normal shyness.

When the Humane Society of Tampa Bay asked for our participation in their children's summer camp program, Debbie M. was happy to oblige. She snatched up volunteers to assist her at the one-week Critter Camp that covers care of animals. Young participants enjoy various arts and crafts and they have opportunities to walk dogs and hold cats. Our topic of horse care would be an addition to their agenda.

Our presentations each week to the revolving eight- to twelve-year-olds encouraged the children to do what they do naturally: notice things and ask questions if something doesn't seem quite right. Teaching them the basic concept that people should be observant because sometimes animals need help would allow them to become the eyes and ears within their communities. They learned to ask, "Where is the water and food?" Some will even specify "clean" water because our philosophy is such that, if we wouldn't drink the water, we shouldn't expect a horse to drink it.

The session was a hit with the Critter Camp children and has become an annual standing event. With Debbie M.'s connections, our children's outreach program continued to evolve. In 2013, she was invited to participate in her school's Great American Teach-in program. Students would rotate through thirty-minute intervals of various presentations.

As always, Debbie M. accepted the challenge and then developed a creative and memorable session to cover her topic of horses. She incorporated a drawing contest into the lesson, during which the artists needed to depict what constitutes proper equine care. Judges at RVR would designate one winner from each class. The coveted prize was an invitation for their families to visit the ranch and an opportunity for the winners to groom Bella, a docile mare.

The artists wooed the judges with their masterpieces. One rule required that the children label the items in their pictures. One of the winners, Isabella, included a jar labeled "medicine (sometimes)" and a sketch of herself brushing and petting a horse, labeled "love/care." Inspired by Debbie M.'s lecture, Isabella later held her own fund-raiser for our horses. When she came to claim her prize of meeting Bella, she donated the $31 she'd earned from her lemonade stand.

Winner Brayden's work of art was splashed with color. It included one black and one brown horse, each labeled "HOS," standing under a bright smiling sun and accompanied by all the things horses need to stay healthy: Hay, Wodr, Gas, Apls, and Carit. He covered all the bases and stole the hearts of the judges. As he took his turn grooming Bella, his beaming smile spoke volumes.

Winner Morgan upped the ante by including a barn, fence, and brush in addition to the food. Her pink horse with navy blue polka dots included a toothy grin from ear to ear. Morgan arrived to claim her prize sporting coordinated pink cowgirl boots, hair ribbon, and tee shirt.

Bella remained still and patient while each contestant showed her the love and care that they had learned horses need. Each grooming session ended with a treat for the precious mare.

As exciting as it is for the young artists to meet a horse, a fringe benefit was that we had the chance to influence the rest of their families during the experience. Each group got a personal tour of the ranch, during which Debbie M.'s commentary about the rescues held the attention of even the littlest visitors.

When explaining the history of each horse, Debbie M. describes the abuse insofar as we know it, because perpetrators aren't generally forthcoming. "Sometimes we don't hear the whole story or the real facts, if people feel like they might get in trouble for telling the truth," she told one group.

"Kind of like in school," one munchkin admitted immediately, drawing chuckles from the adults. His comical comment rang insightfully true.

Later, one boy became desperate to get Debbie M.'s attention while she told the story of our bald-faced Cowboy. "Mrs. M.," he repeated incessantly, with his hand waving about in the air.

"Yes?" Debbie M. answered after she finished her explanation.

"Cowboy pooped," the observant winner announced, triggering another round of laughter.

"Oh good!" Debbie M. replied. "That means he's healthy. You should see how excited people get around here to see poop!"

Another youngster was thoroughly impressed by Debbie M.'s extensive knowledge. "Miss M., when you first got here, did you know everything?" he asked.

"Oh, my gosh, no! I'm still learning every day," she admitted.

The Great American Teach-in event proved to be a resounding success, and Debbie M. was later approached by a teacher from the second grade's gifted program. As animal lovers, the two women bonded over their common interest. The teacher asked Debbie M. to meet with a student who wanted to learn more about horses.

On their agreed-upon date, Debbie M. joined Cami in her classroom for an interview. Among other questions, Cami asked her, "What does a horse feel like?"

Confused, Debbie M. attempted to clarify. "Do you mean their feelings, or what one would feel like if you touched it?"

"If you touched it," Cami replied. She'd never felt one.

At the conclusion of the interview, Debbie M. invited Cami and her family to the upcoming Justice 4 Mustangs fundraiser, grabbing another opportunity to spread our message further.

*Desensitizing, or "de-spooking," a horse,
teaches the horse not to panic when exposed
to certain objects or experiences.
Inexperienced horses need to be desensitized
to the halter and saddle before they can be
ridden, but even mature horses are often
spooked by plastic bags, bouncing rubber
balls, or loud traffic sounds.*[30]

CHAPTER 24

Our educational program was gaining traction and I was thrilled we were proactively arming the next generation of pet owners and policy makers. Each time I look at an incoming rescue, I feel the seeds we are planting cannot grow fast enough.

Upon their arrival at the ranch, many horses are fighting for survival. Their true personalities may be tucked beneath the pain and suffering. Even after a several-month-long rehabilitation, they still might not show their true spirit. But once they're fattened up and healthy again, the fire, fight, and passion reemerge.

At that point, the rehabilitated horses are ready for adoption, but we still face a major obstacle. Many families are in search of a horse to ride, so an unknown riding temperament can be a deterrent to adoption. If we could showcase the rideable horses, it would facilitate quicker and more adoptions.

One lesson I've learned the hard way is that the riding temperament can only be experienced, not predicted. Our work with the animals during their rehabilitation provides no indicator

---

[30] WikiHow. "How to Desensitize a Horse."
www.wikihow.com/Desensitize-a-Horse (accessed 8/22/15).

as to whether they're green—that is, untrained—or if they're dead broke, meaning kid-proof.

Sometimes a pathetically skinny horse will perform amazing trick moves once it's plumped back to size. Another horse I'd assume was trained because it's so sweet on the ground might go for blood under saddle. But potential adoptive families aren't willing to adopt an animal on a coin toss. If the intention of the adoption is to ride, they need to be certain about the riding personality.

I assessed each horse as accurately as I could, but I was being pulled in so many directions that my time for any particular task was increasingly limited. Besides, riding any of the rescues had never been a priority or plan.

As I watched Sergio, the trainer, working with Marcy and her horse in the paddock, an idea sprung to mind. Sergio was a superb horseman and used a firm but humane style with the animals, which I call a "rainbows and butterflies" approach. His evaluation of our horses' riding temperaments could make him a valuable asset to our team.

I began by asking Sergio to assess some recently rehabilitated horses to determine what they knew and how they handled under saddle. He jumped at the challenge and became my new crash test dummy. His persistence in working with his ornery childhood devil, Spartacus, had honed his intuition and instincts.

After Spartacus flung Sergio off like a ragdoll, leaving him crumpled and gasping for breath, Sergio perfected a vice grip hold that generally prevents him from being thrown. His technique earned him a fitting nickname: the Flea.

Spartacus had provided his master many hours of practice when it came to reading the early warning signs of a throw. When Sergio feels the imminent buck, he asks the horse to do something unexpected, like go in a circle. The distraction snaps the horse's attention back to the task at hand, and typically precludes the buck. Many riders' knee-jerk reaction is to panic and grab the saddle for dear life, which further encourages the throw. Sergio's been dismounted plenty of times, but his savvy technique of falling has prevented injury.

With Sergio's guidance, our horses were categorized into those suitable for children, those that were extremely dangerous and should be reserved as a pasture ornament, and everything in between. Knowledge of the riding temperament and ability allowed us to better match a horse and owner, based on their complimentary skill levels. Photos or videos of Sergio riding any horse fast-tracked its adoption. The addition of my crash test dummy was a great success.

Sergio's reputation at the ranch grew and adoptive parents began using him as a personal trainer. His knack for assessing the root cause of a horse's unwanted behavior and instructing the handler how to correct the problem won him many more supporters.

As our involvement with children increased, I needed help ascertaining which horses had the propensity and tolerance for the little ones. In these evaluations, Sergio pushes the equine buttons, while also looking for basic obedience signals, such as an immediate response to "whoa" and "back." In ever-increasing challenges, he tests the reaction to unfamiliar or uncomfortable situations, searching for the animal's limits. Each attempt to fluster the horse is performed humanely and taken very carefully.

We were ramping up for an important fund-raiser in support of the American Wild Horse Preservation Campaign. The Justice 4 Mustangs fund-raiser would raise awareness of the national conundrum of wild mustangs. In the open fields across the country, mustang horses roam alongside cattle and other wild species. A common misconception is that all the animals roam freely and peacefully on the rolling plains, but that's not exactly true.

As cattle farmers jockey for suitable land, they contend that the wild mustangs compromise their livelihood by infringing on the cows' food. The actual impact to the farmers is a national debate, with staunch supporters on either side of the argument. In any case, the Bureau of Land Management (BLM) is the government agency responsible for overseeing the public lands.

In response to complaints of nuisance wild mustangs, the BLM rounds up the culprits using either helicopters or bait to capture them. What is the fate of these horses? The fortunate few are moved into adoptive homes, but the vast majority aren't.

At the Justice 4 Mustangs fund-raiser we would showcase Horace, our branded and tattooed full mustang. He could help us raise awareness of the plight of his breed, but we needed to ensure he was a well-behaved ambassador because he would be coming into contact with children. Our student Cami and her family were already looking forward to meeting him.

We enrolled Horace in Sergio's boot camp for a heavy desensitization assignment. Horace had been born in captivity and was familiar with human handling, so he wasn't as wild as if he'd been freshly rounded up from the plains.

The drill sergeant ran his new recruit through rigorous obstacles. Sergio walked Horace through a kiddie pool of empty water bottles and placed a tarp over his head, then waited patiently until Horace became soothed and quiet. They entered the pond to a depth that reached Horace's neck. Sergio cracked a bull whip nearby. Each test was an attempt to set off our mustang in a controlled environment, but nothing fazed our boy. Horace aced boot camp and was ready for his big debut.

> *Research has confirmed the effectiveness of equine therapy, showing that it lowers blood pressure and heart rate, alleviates stress, and reduces symptoms of anxiety and depression.*[31]

CHAPTER 25

We were completing our due diligence to ensure the safety of the children who would be coming into contact with Horace. With children as a critical component of our long-term success, we attempt to incorporate them into our programs as much as possible. Especially beneficial are the children who are raised among horses.

As any parent can attest, raising a child is one of the most rewarding as well as one of the most challenging experiences one can undertake. Parents committed to exposing their children to horses generally find that the animals provide significant enrichment to their children's lives. Any caring parent wants the best for their children, and when a child possesses any learning or emotional challenges, those parents would move mountains to improve their child's quality of life. Sometimes it takes trial and error before landing on just the right solution, but persistence usually pays off.

Kelly and her husband, Randall, are two such caring parents. Their eleven-year-old daughter, Jillian, was struggling. Her dyslexia had created learning challenges, which led to enormous stress for the entire family, and finally manifested in debilitating anxiety for Jillian, even to the point of suicidal

---

[31] Elements Behavioral Health. "5 Lessons People Can Learn from Horses in Equine Therapy." www.elementsbehavioralhealth.com/addiction-treatment/lessons-equine-therapy/ (accessed 8/22/15).

thoughts. Traditional medications only exacerbated her condition, making Kelly and Randall more desperate to reach their suffering girl.

When Jillian was first diagnosed with dyslexia, Kelly realized that her daughter's learning challenges might preclude a college education, given that school was already a source of immense pressure. She considered how she and Randall might instill in Jillian a talent that could potentially be built upon one day as a career. If college worked out, great, but if not, then they wouldn't be scrambling for a plan when Jillian graduated from high school.

Kelly always believed that interacting with four-legged friends taught children compassion and valuable life lessons. Although the experiences might end painfully, caring for animals is typically rewarding for anyone, especially children.

Jillian has an innate gift that extends well beyond the normal joy of working with animals. So Kelly considered opportunities that would expose Jillian to some furry buddies. The family had fostered dogs, but kept falling in love with each one. Their dog-fostering career finally ended when their family pooch became elderly and infirm. Old Scout needed peace and solitude, not another spastic foster dog pestering him.

Over the years, Jillian's condition became more debilitating, making Kelly more desperate for a solution. She recalled the enjoyment horseback-riding lessons brought Jillian for two summers, years earlier. With that in mind, her maternal instinct led her to RVR.

The pair began to volunteer together, and while Kelly enjoyed all the horses on an equal and ordinary basis, Jillian developed an instant and electric attraction to Horace. He responded in kind. No one could hold a candle to her Horace. She loved the fact that the adorable mustang from the wild was unique, but more than anything, their connection escaped words.

It just *was*. Horace clearly enjoyed Jillian's company and he demonstrated a tremendous amount of patience with her.

To Jillian, it felt like a match made in heaven and she begged her parents to adopt Horace. But Kelly and Randall had no plans for adopting any horse, especially not one that came with a companion, namely Bella. Bella and Horace had been delivered to us as a pair and we intended to adopt them out that way.

Soon after, another volunteer stepped up to adopt both Horace and Bella. Although the new owner's real interest and attraction was with Bella, she had agreed to adopt Horace as part of the deal. Naturally, Jillian was distraught at the thought of losing her best friend, but to her relief, Horace and Bella remained at RVR as boarders after their adoption. Their new owner kindly allowed Jillian to continue hanging out with her buddy, Horace, and the additional time spent together further cemented their bond.

During their time at RVR, Horace and Bella had both established new friendships with other RVR pasture mates. When their adoptive mom later decided she could no longer keep Horace, he was placed back up for adoption, to my dismay. This time he would be available as a single, rather than as half of a duo. By this time, both Horace and Bella had established other friendships among their herd, so keeping them together was no longer critical.

With this change of events, Kelly and Randall succumbed to Jillian's *"Please! Please! Please!"* Although they had never imagined or intended on getting a horse, they adopted Horace, to their daughter's delight.

For the adoption celebration, Kelly wanted to honor a key aspect of Jillian's Kazakhstani heritage. Kazakhstan is home to ancient Mongolian horse tribes who live on the plains of Siberia and central Asia. Mongols are credited as the first to tame wild horses. Today, horses are still central to the culture in Kazakhstan, where all the children learn how to ride and an elaborate celebration commemorates a child receiving his first horse. In the native land, the partygoers play games on horseback and perform other rituals that Kelly wouldn't be able to duplicate, but she wanted a similar celebration.

For their local adoption event, Kelly coordinated a potluck dinner for forty RVR friends. At the party, Jillian glowed, wearing a replica of the national Kazakhstan costume. Gold scrolls decorated the long, bright red vest she wore over her flowing white gown. A matching red cap, adorned with similar scrolls, was topped with a bushy white fluff of feathers. Long brown braids hung from either side of the fancy cap.

Although Kelly and Randall legally signed Horace's adoption papers, it was important to them that Jillian also pledge a formal commitment to her horse. Kelly printed a copy of a poem, titled "Forever Horse," which Jillian read to the group while Horace nuzzled his forever-girl. Jillian and I both signed the printout of the poem, solidifying her personal commitment to both Horace and me. It read:

FOREVER HORSE

Before you consider or think about adopting me, realize that I am a
FOREVER HORSE.
I am not an until you get bored or lose interest in me horse.
I am not an until you go off to college or find boys instead horse.
I am not an until I get old horse.
I am not an until I get lame horse.
I am not an until you have to move horse.

I am not an until you get a new, younger horse horse.

I am not an until you get pregnant horse.

I am a FOREVER HORSE.

If you cannot promise FOREVER,

I am not your horse.

I have already been through too much.

(Author unknown)

Horsemanship is literally and figuratively in Jillian's blood. Her parents are fully committed to ensuring she is a competent rider and horse owner. Because they don't have horse experience, they hired Sergio to help Jillian. It's a perfect match because Sergio possesses a genuine knack for working with children. His constant flowing feedback is easy for a child to understand, and his patience for repetition is commendable.

Sergio and Jillian began with the basics. Jillian needed to learn how to work with her horse from the ground up. Not only did Sergio teach her all the aspects of horsemanship, he groomed her to be a confident and capable owner.

When the novelty of their relationship wore off, Horace and Jillian reached a difficult working phase. When the stubborn giant began testing his impatient girl, Sergio's goal was to establish Jillian as Horace's boss. The power struggle presented a healthy challenge that helped Jillian grow.

Lunging is one method Sergio used to help Jillian assert herself as dominant over her horse. This practice requires her to run Horace in a circle around her using a lead line along with voice and body commands. Jillian controls the speed and direction of the horse. Not only does this exercise establish leadership, it instills cooperation between horse and human.

A lunging training session with Sergio prompts a barrage of feedback:

"Now don't pull on the rope—hold it. If he pulls on it, give it a little snap. . . . Watch what happens to the rope: saggy here and stretched out there. . . . So right now I want you to step in on him. Not step in front of him, step in on him. You're taking a big step in front of him—look at me. What I meant was step up and push him away with your body. Try it again . . . Good . . . Now hold your distance. Don't do anything. Practice giving your verbal cues. Do you hear when I click? Do it when I do it. . . . Horses are very repetitive, so figure out what he does in the first couple circles and that's what he's going to keep doing. . . . The rope's really saggy right there, it means he came in on you. . . . Ask him to step up the pace, use verbal cues." And so on and so on.

At times, Jillian's frustration bubbles to the surface, but she's a tough little cookie. She keeps working on it. She constantly tweaks her method as her teacher pushes her to attain a high standard.

After Jillian and Horace complete their exercises to Sergio's satisfaction, Jillian's reward is riding her boy. It's by far her favorite part of the lesson.

Still, Sergio insists on the rainbows-and-butterflies approach that we request of him. When Jillian gives a hard pull to turn Horace around, Sergio corrects her immediately.

"You need to be more gentle," he tells her. "When he wasn't being nice to you earlier, it's okay to give him a firm correction, but when he's being nice to you, like he is now, you need to be nice and gentle with him." Every bit of feedback, every correction, and every request brings Jillian one step closer to being a competent and confident horse owner.

The two begin to move as one as they cruise lap after lap around the paddock. Still, Sergio insists on improving Jillian's method, and with his guidance, suddenly Jillian's bouncy posture transforms into a smooth steady glide. It's a wonderful sight to behold. The pretty waif controls her thousand-pound machine effortlessly.

"Perfect!" Sergio encourages. "That looks beautiful."

His words are music to Jillian's and Kelly's ears.

Finally, the knots that had taken up residence in Kelly's gut have begun to loosen. The transformation Jillian has undergone by working with the horses, and Horace specifically, is just what Kelly had hoped. She sees relaxation in her daughter now. And, finally, enjoyment. Jillian's genuine laughter has returned, replacing the forced, fake anxious one that had become her norm. Her desire to connect with the horses, rather than remain withdrawn in her world of solitude, indicates significant progress.

Jillian generally finds it difficult to express her feelings, but she found a way to communicate the benefit that Horace and the other RVR horses have brought her. "This is where I feel relaxed and happy," she told Kelly. "The horses understand me."

> *Children are the world's most valuable*
> *resource and its best hope for the future.*
>
> —*John F. Kennedy*

CHAPTER 26

Sergio's work with Horace in preparation for our Justice 4 Mustangs fund-raiser was a success. On the day of the event, the gentle giant cooperated fully with Cami, who carried her pad and pencil to take note of any new facts. Not only did the little blonde pixie get to touch a horse for the first time, but our handsome fellow gave Cami her first horseback ride.

"You owe me for this!" Debbie M. teased the beaming girl. Cami's sincere interest in and enthusiasm for horses impressed Debbie M. and she hatched an idea to include Cami in an educational outreach program.

"I'd really like you to help me," Debbie M. told her budding protégé. She had visions of Cami assisting in some fashion with the next Great American Teach-in, but then considered Cami's shyness and thought perhaps she wouldn't be willing. Surprisingly, Cami was excited about being involved, and after her teacher and parents consented, they formed a plan.

In the meantime, Debbie M. rallied her RVR team for the upcoming event. Having observed Alyssa's love of children and her innate teaching ability, Debbie M. invited her to the Great American Teach-in. Alyssa rose to the challenge, further expanding her résumé. With a team made up of three powerhouses, Debbie M., Charity, and Alyssa were armed to spread a whole lot of C.L.E.A.R.

On the day of the event, Cami was excused from her class to attend Debbie M.'s presentation to a group of students in another room. When Cami left her classroom, her teacher had the remaining students write down their questions about horses on Post-it notes. Afterward, they stuck the pile on Cami's desk.

Cami retrieved the sticky notes, then rejoined Debbie M., Charity, and Alyssa for a working lunch to review the questions from Cami's classmates. Cami read each note to the RVR experts and jotted down their answers. Then during the session in her classroom, Cami read the questions and answers to her friends. Shy Cami blossomed as she nailed her first equine presentation. Her proud mother was there to witness the special occasion.

Sometimes it's difficult to read what a person is thinking, but Cami made it easy for Debbie M. when she told her, "I want to do that again next year!" In addition to their success with Cami, the RVR gang presented to twenty-two classes, altogether consisting of 280 students in one day, doubling the prior year's reach.

The latest works of art were judged back at the ranch and each was heartfelt and adorable. As one girl wrote, "Thank you for telling us amazing facts about horses . . . now me and my friends all want to help horses and we love them very much." She had colored a blond figurine that represented herself, with a speech bubble that said, "We help horses." However, the unicorn with an injured leg had a question for her: "But do you help unicorns?"

Even the youngest audience understood our message, as one six-year-old proved. "Horsis need wotr if horsis dont git wotr they will git D-hidratide and maby diye!"

Besides being priceless, every depiction validated that our message to the children was taking hold. Our RVR educators were making significant inroads with the children, and as our educational leader, Debbie M. has taken her role to heart and performs it beautifully. She seizes every forum and each daily interaction as an opportunity to increase awareness. Her creative methods recruit children to become instruments of change.

Before the long Thanksgiving holiday weekend, she gave her students a suggestion. "Next week is Thanksgiving. When you're having dinner with all those people, tell them everything you learned about horses and then they will know, too."

This example and all the other outreach methods Debbie M. and our C.L.E.A.R team use to imprint the children come back to us in wonderful ways, validating our work. In one case, first-grader Morgan completed her nonfiction essay during an in-class writing assignment. The teacher milled about the room as the fledgling authors scribbled out their stories. From overhead, she scanned Morgan's work, then told her that although her story was sweet, she couldn't use make believe for the assignment. Her description about a horse whose best friend was a donkey was a cute work of fiction.

Morgan's mother later defended her daughter to the teacher. "No, it's not her imagination. She's met the horse and donkey. They live at RVR!"

Morgan remembered Debbie M.'s presentation, specifically when she said, "We have a horse who has her own pet," referring to our first girl, Charity. The old mare was glued at the hip to Dominick the donkey. She later adopted his mom, Rosita, and her son, Christian, to round out her personal herd. That one statement stuck with Morgan—that a horse could have a friend and that it could be a donkey. This kind of feedback melts our hearts and confirms that what we do leaves a lasting impression.

A core element of our educational curriculum includes the basics of horse care. For many people, the dream of owning a horse is an enjoyable fantasy, but the financial and care commitments could shock or overwhelm those who take the plunge without sufficient awareness. Many of our rescues come from owners who are in over their heads financially. Informing oneself prior to making decisions about horse ownership prevents later neglect.

First, people interested in buying or adopting a horse should consider the routine cost. The average monthly expense to care for one is about $500, which would include trimming of their hooves every six weeks, a job for the farrier. If shoes are required, it adds another $120 to $250 per six-week treatment. Without proper foot care, serious issues can arise, such as we saw with our wild child, Destiny. Her previous owner neglected her hooves, which cracked, split, and became deformed, leaving Destiny in constant pain. After months of work, her hooves finally healed and the supplements she was given allowed them to grow healthier.

In addition to routine hoof care, annual dental care is also to be expected. A horse's teeth continually emerge from the gumline for most of its adult life. Their upper and lower jaws are unequal widths, creating a misalignment. Accordingly, the teeth of horses in captivity do not naturally grind to a flat chewing surface like they do in the wild, where the movements of grazing for survival prevent the issue.

If the teeth of captive horses are left unattended, a jagged tooth pattern results and impairs the ability to chew food, hampering the digestive system and leading to significant health problems. A 100-dollar annual filing of the chewing surface, a procedure called floating, is performed by an equine dentist and keeps that situation in check.

In addition to routine care, owners who board their horses at a facility can pay an additional several hundred dollars a month. With all these ongoing costs in consideration, even a "free" horse is hardly free.

Our amazing C.L.E.A.R educators continually increase the breadth of our influence to create more voices for the voiceless. We toss our little pebbles into the water and watch the expanding ripple.

By nature, horses instinctively seek leadership. . . . When a naturally submissive horse has to deal with an owner who does not lead, this horse tries to be the more dominant one, or even to be the leader.[32]

CHAPTER 27

We were making progress on many fronts, and our expanding influence in the community led to an increase in our volunteer base. As our band of Angels grew, it just so happened that the great majority were women. The handful of men we attract round out our diverse team.

One of our guys hails from the cattle ranches of eastern Oregon. As a child, David considered horses to be more like transportation, such as bicycles, than beautiful living beings. He paid no mind to learning proper horsemanship or establishing a relationship with any animal he encountered. Once he moved away from home, he never gave horses a second thought.

In adulthood, David's prestigious career in army intelligence landed him tours in war-torn Iraq and Afghanistan, before he finally settled in Washington, D.C. The deployments separated him from his baby girl, Bethany, and a breakup with Bethany's mother several years later ensured he'd see his daughter even less.

David had recently retired from the military when Bethany's mother relocated with her daughter to Florida. David followed. His career had already cost him too much precious time with his girl. Determined to make the most of every hour spent

---

[32] Straightness Training. "13 Ways to Establish and Confirm Leadership." http://straightnesstraining.com/the-rider/horsemanship/be-the-leader-with-your-horse/ (accessed 8/23/15).

together, David brainstormed various activities he and Bethany could do as a team in their new city.

A television advertisement about RVR led them to us. With his background on a farming ranch, David was experienced building fences, fixing "ranch things" such as stalls and gates, and driving a tractor. He envisioned lending us a hand while we brought him back to his roots. Plus, it would be a wonderful bonding activity and an enriching experience for Bethany.

Soon after they began volunteering, David developed an appreciation for the majestic beauties that he never felt as a child. He became eager to learn about equine behaviors, how to develop a bond with a horse, and how to earn their respect. He realized that a balanced relationship requires the human to become a strong, consistent leader—a skill he believed would benefit Bethany for the rest of her life. Adopting a horse would teach his daughter life lessons as well as provide a bonding opportunity for the pair. Of course, the blond preteen was elated with her father's suggestion and they set off to find a special horse.

If Bethany had gotten her way, they would have adopted every available animal at the ranch. Although ownership hadn't been David's original plan, he took a shining to an old, lazy quarter horse named Rojo. The mellow fellow seemed to be a good starter horse for Bethany and she was thrilled upon his adoption.

Father and daughter took their first riding lesson on the same day. With Sergio as their mentor, the duo were off to a quick start with their new horse. Soon, however, Mr. Rojo Grumpypants got very grouchy when David tried to lunge him. This situation was beyond his level of expertise, which was practically nonexistent, and so David reached out for help from an unlikely place: his church.

Held at the Florida State Fairgrounds, the Cowboy-Up Ministry is run by a seasoned cowboy and horse trainer named

Skipper. During each session, Skipper preaches a Christian message while training a wayward horse. Upon David's request, he and Rojo were selected to work with Skipper in front of the congregation, where David demonstrated his complete lack of cowboy skills to the two hundred onlookers. Bethany cringed from the sidelines. After proving to the crowd that Rojo was uncontrollable, David handed the lead to Skipper. Within moments of being under the expert's command, Rojo transformed into an obedient superstar.

The humbling experience was an eye-opener for David. The handler made all the difference. One hundred percent. The source of their problem was David, not Rojo. That realization smacked David between the eyes. Leadership seemed to be the critical component. You can't cheat on it and there are no shortcuts. His embarrassing failure on center stage was a huge turning point for David, and he and Bethany committed to stepping up their game.

With renewed enthusiasm and improved leadership skills, David and Bethany found greater success with Rojo. The pair was ready for a second horse. Feisty April had been adopted out once already, with Rojo, and they were later returned to us. Because the horses had established a relationship with each other already, April was the natural choice for David. After Sergio's evaluation of the spunky girl, he gave her two thumbs up. "There's nothing mean about her," he told David. The spirited mare suited the dad and mellow Rojo suited the daughter. April's adoption was finalized soon after.

David and Bethany began trail-riding together, and their routine included crossing a fallen tree. This simple practice helped them establish leadership and trust with their horses.

One day, instead of stepping over the fallen log, Rojo jumped over, to Bethany's delight. One little taste of a trick and she was hooked. But the jump was a fluke for stubborn, old Rojo and Bethany wasn't able to get him to repeat it, to her great dismay. But sprightly April was willing and eager. Bethany quickly hijacked her father's horse and began jumping the log with April. She and her mare now run circles around David and Rojo, and Bethany is itching for more tricks. Her experiences have convinced her that her future career needs to include horses in some way.

David and Bethany are permanent fixtures at the ranch. Their commitment to each other is a refreshing and heartwarming example to witness, and it demonstrates what a true bonding experience between a father and child can be.

Besides the camaraderie and the enjoyment of the horses, their involvement at RVR has taught both David and Bethany tough life lessons by witnessing the end of life for many horses. David stepped into a heartbreaking but critical role at the ranch. He's one of our team members who perform the burials of our precious babies after they cross the rainbow bridge.

When our rescues arrive, they have seen the worst of humanity and then we shower them with the best of humanity. The golden treatment continues through till the end of their lives, when a loving group comforts and guides the fallen horses across the bridge, and even beyond.

The burial grounds are a peaceful and serene field, past the pond, near the back of the property. The open expanse of land is carpeted in brush and speckled with trees. Sunshine pours through the fresh air and the distant treeline frames the perimeter.

Brilliant flowers adorn the graves of the recently fallen, such as my first rescue baby, Charity. When we removed the battered mare from her torture, we were able to provide her ten peaceful years and a best buddy named Dominick before the pain in her old weary bones became too much to bear.

When David placed Charity in her final resting place he was reminded of the 23rd Psalm. It brings him peace each time he delivers a soul to the field.

> *The Lord is my shepherd; I shall not want.*
> *He makes me lie down in green pastures.*
> *He leads me beside still waters.*

Rest in peace, Sweet Charity.

The number one distinguishing factor between horses and ponies is height. Traditionally, any adult animal shorter than 14.2 hands high (58 inches) is considered a pony.[33]

CHAPTER 28

Although David's role in the burial process is a particularly heart-wrenching one, many aspects of what we do are emotionally taxing. But God keeps providing me with people who don't back away from a tough challenge.

Take Debbie, for instance. Debbie S. got her first pony at the age of three and grew up bouncing in the saddle. As an adult, she specialized in the competitive hunter jumper sport until one fateful show when her horse faltered on a jump.

He needed to clear a four-foot-high fence that straddled water. Perhaps the shimmering movement or the glistening lights reflecting off the rippled surface startled him. He started to go, but then Debbie S. felt him refuse. By that time she'd already committed and was launching forward. Her horse then decided to complete the jump, except his rhythm was broken and Debbie S. crashed to the ground. Unable to speak and frozen in place by having the wind knocked out of her, Debbie S. was whisked by a Bayflite helicopter to the hospital, per show protocol.

Her doctor didn't mince words when he lit into her over her hobby and how it continued to result in soft tissue injuries. "So you got back on the horses and here we are again," he said

---

[33] Five Oaks Riding Stables. "What is the Difference Between a Horse and a Pony?" January 24, 2014.
http://www.fiveoaksridingstables.com/blog/difference-horse-pony/ (accessed 8/23/15).

sternly. "You can't do this anymore. I can't keep you away from horses, but you might not walk if this happens again."

Debbie S.'s previous injury should have ended her jumping career, but she'd been stubborn. This time was really the end of it.

Staying with the horse theme, she switched gears and began an after-school riding academy that focused on the fine art of dressage. Business flourished until the economy crashed and dragged her facility down with it. Debbie S. found herself in the dreadful position of rehoming her horses.

With the loss of her business and the animals that she loved, Debbie S. needed something to patch her broken heart and fill the empty hours, so she volunteered at a soup kitchen and animal shelter. Those opportunities killed time, but they weren't bringing her heart joy.

Finally, her friend from work mentioned RVR and Debbie S.'s heart skipped a beat at the idea of working with horses again. She was amazed to learn we were right around the corner from her home.

Debbie S. was overwhelmed when she first joined our team. In all her years of working with horses, she'd never seen any battered or emaciated. Being around horses again and helping those so desperately in need soothed her ragged soul.

She was completely content to just scoop poop and fill water buckets, but we knew she was an experienced horsewoman, so we razzed her about getting one of her own. "They're all mine," she would tell us. "Each one has a little piece of me."

Late one Sunday evening in December, Debbie S.'s friend called. Her daughter had spotted a hurt horse from the road and stopped to take a picture. It was a baby bleeding from injuries. A full-grown cattle collar intended for a 1,500-pound cow hung from the thin neck of the tiny filly. The heavy grate dug into her ribs for support. A bloody pulp oozed where the hoof should have been. Her injury was apparently the reason for the collar.

"Send me the address," I instructed after Debbie S. gave me the lowdown.

I'd been on edge all day, fixated on Rojo. An unsettled feeling weighed me down, but I couldn't pinpoint what it was. Pacing didn't bring me any answers.

My gut insisted that something was wrong with him, but I stood watching him in the round pen and could clearly see he was fine. Yet the nagging feeling was relentless. The instant Debbie S. gave me the address of the hurt filly, it struck me: My angst over Rojo hadn't actually been about him, but about the people who abused him. Another horse had fallen into the same cruel hands.

"The address is *what?*" I asked Debbie S. in disbelief. Rojo's abusers had done it again and I was infuriated.

Kit and I jumped in the truck and Debbie S. joined us, since she was the one who had received the tip. When we arrived on the scene, it was all too familiar. Let's just say our prior encounter hadn't gone smoothly.

The owner was adamant about not letting us on the property. He hadn't forgotten the last encounter either. The exchange heated to a boil in an instant.

As the newcomer, Debbie S. stepped in to diffuse the ticking time bomb.

"Sir, I don't know what happened in the past, but I just want to check out your little filly. I just want to help the horse, I don't want to get any sheriffs involved." Her gentle approach calmed the agitated man.

"I like you," the man told her. "You can come with me." And he led her onto the property in search of the girl we later named Angel.

When Debbie S. spotted the baby on the ground, she thought Angel was already gone, but then she saw faint movement. Debbie S. realized the poor weak baby couldn't get up because of the ludicrous grate around her neck.

The owner explained, "We've been putting peroxide on her wound and used the collar to prevent her from reaching her hoof."

Debbie S. wanted to grab the man by the shoulders to try shaking sense into him, but her softer approach had gotten her onto the property. She needed to maintain her cool.

"Okay," she said, as if she was in full agreement with his ridiculous treatment plan. "But she needs a vet. We need to help her." Finally, the man consented to let us help and he began to prod the fallen girl to walk to the road where Kit and I waited.

"No, we're going to carry her," Debbie S. firmly insisted. The 100 pounds of Shetland pony baby was no problem for the two of them to manage.

When they arrived to the front of the property, the scene heated up again as soon as the man saw the awaiting sheriff.

"You said you wouldn't call the police," the man spat.

"I didn't call and we just want to help the horse," Debbie S. replied calmly, playing her role of good cop perfectly.

Speaking Spanish, I jumped into a conversation with the man and his wife, who had joined us, trying to meet them on common ground to gain their cooperation.

Meanwhile, the sheriff, who knew nothing about horses, agreed that Angel needed help and convinced the couple to allow us to bring Angel for a medical evaluation.

The owners insisted they wanted to help, so they followed us to the vet. The test results proved bleak. Contagious swamp fever and rampant septic in her system was decimating poor Angel. A possible surgery was very radical and had only a 50 percent chance of success. With the vet's recommendation, we authorized him to end her life peacefully.

Angel's owners, who had been so insistent that they wanted to help her, didn't even elect to bury their little girl. So Angel came home to RVR for her final resting place among loving people and fellow horses.

Angel is our rescue baby who didn't make it back alive, but we were able to shower love and affection on her for the final few minutes of her short life. We can't save them all, but we certainly make whatever difference we can in each situation.

> *Horse height is measured from the ground to*
> *the withers in a four-inch unit called hands.*
> *This distance remains constant, whereas the*
> *height to the top of the head varies depending*
> *on the angle of the neck.*

CHAPTER 29

In the world of horse rescue, we see horrific cases of neglect and abuse, like Angel and so many others. The general public doesn't typically get a glimpse into this world, as evidenced by nearly 100 percent of our volunteers who never knew the need for rescue existed until they walked through our gates.

What the world most commonly sees is the glamour of Thoroughbred racing. Even most "non-horse" people are familiar with the sport sometimes known as the "rich man's hobby," where compact jockeys atop beasts bred for speed vie for the lead in the pack.

The practice is the same at racetracks throughout the country, although some tracks have the notorious glitz and glamour while others are threadbare. At the opening bell, a stampede of contenders charges out of the gates, carrying their expert riders.

"And they're off," the announcer bellows over the loudspeakers, and then continues to rattle off details of the unfolding race.[34] On April 20, 2008, at Tampa Bay Downs, Waving Monarch broke for the lead from the outside, but quickly fell into second place behind Kin Kon. He charged along nosing Kin Kon's tail, until the far turn. Waving Monarch crept forward,

---

[34] RVR Horse Rescue's YouTube Channel. "Waving Monarch's Story: Victory, Despair & Rebirth." December 16, 2014. www.youtube.com/watch?v=SVyAqgj7mVc (accessed 8/23/15).

passing on the outside and reaching a nose ahead by the time they rounded the turn and began the final stretch. On the straightaway, he never looked back and literally left the rest of the field in his dust as he flew across the finish line.

Waving Monarch was bred at a reputable horse farm in Kentucky, sired by Wavering Monarch and his beautiful dam, Widow's Walk. Their offspring, a chestnut gelding adorned with a white star on his face, was nearing the end of his successful career when he surged to victory at Tampa Bay Downs. Waving Monarch earned a decent $100,000 by winning or placing in eleven of his seventeen starts. Although he performed respectably, his earnings were a far cry from the $450,000 his prominent father amassed.[35]

Waving Monarch raced at Calder in Miami and Tampa Bay Downs, living in the lap of equine luxury. Any active Thoroughbred dines on gourmet food and gets top-notch care, all of which quickly disappears when their career wanes. Once Waving Monarch stopped making money, he began to plod down the controversial path of many retired Thoroughbreds. In his case, Monarch was more fortunate than many and was taken in by a kind elderly gentleman. The new owner provided a safe and secure second home for the retired racer, and in return, Monarch provided trail rides for the man.

The gentle soul began to slide down a slippery slope into increasingly unsuitable circumstances when the man could no longer care for him. He hit rock bottom when he landed in a junkyard disguised as a farm outside Plant City. Monarch had no food or hay and only nasty stagnant green water. His pasture mates were rusty discarded appliances and trash. He attempted to stay alive by eating the dirt he stood on.

---

[35] Pedigree Online Thoroughbred Database.
www.pedigreequery.com/wavering+monarch (accessed 8/23/15).

In 2011, just three years after his stunning victories, the once spunky muscular machine was merely a shadow of his original self. By the time his RVR Angels saved him, skin hung off his bony sunken frame. His once shiny coat was dull and faded. His spirit was broken and sadness dripped from his dark eyes.

I honestly thought he was too far gone and I still can't believe he survived. His incredible will to live was the only thing that saved him.

After his rehabilitation, Monarch was adopted into a loving home, then tragically, nearly three years later, we got the call. Due to a crisis within Monarch's family, they needed to return the chestnut beauty. The call disappointed everyone, and maddened some.

But, as the saying goes, shit happens. People get sick or fall into financial straits or any number of catastrophic events that can make an owner need to rehome an animal. Our adoption contract requires the adoptive owner to contact us if the need to relinquish the horse ever arises. It's our way to ensure these horses, who've already been to hell and back, don't return to hell. It doesn't guarantee we'll be in a position to take back every horse, but so far we've been able to handle the few who needed to be returned. Monarch will have a home with us until another family finds him.

His story is one tragic example of the controversial horse-racing business. I'm not inherently opposed to Thoroughbred racing. But I am opposed to the inhumane treatment of the animals and the disposing of them as garbage once they no longer serve a useful purpose on the track. Sometimes we pick up dilapidated Thoroughbred rescues off the streets, like Monarch, but sometimes we have the opportunity to help before the situation becomes as dire as Monarch's.

Because of our proximity to the Tampa Downs racetrack and our affiliation with their veterinarian, we get a glimpse into this high stakes world that we might not otherwise see. Sometimes our connection allows us to pluck rescues directly from the track, as we did in the case of Frenchie and Mason.

The fate of an injured racehorse is never good. So, when Dr. Gold alerted us to a wounded racer named Frenchie, we met at the track to check him out. During our evaluation of Frenchie, one of the track staffers mentioned that it was Mason's last day. The poor boy was scheduled to be euthanized due to his non–life threatening leg injury. After a quick peek at Mason, we decided to take him as well as Frenchie.

Mason and Frenchie both went on to be adopted into loving homes and both still reside at RVR as boarders. These two Thoroughbreds were fortunate not to become another fatal statistic. It's tragic that injured racers are put down, although a common alternative is the slaughterhouse, which is even worse. There's no good solution to humanely handle the volume of retired Thoroughbreds.

Every once in a while we come across reputable racing owners who legitimately attempt to place a retired animal into a loving home rather than opt for euthanasia or slaughter. One day we were asked to take a horse whose bleeding capillaries had ended his racing career. His injury was treated by scraping and searing the blown-out capillaries. X-rays were taken, and his feet were treated. All these procedures were medical expenses that the owner wouldn't recoup, but electing to have them done demonstrated their true compassion. Many owners would have dumped him, but this owner did right by the dark bay gelding, who shimmers in a glossy jet-black. They delivered the four-year-old to us and left a bag of feed, as well, becoming one of the most caring experiences with a Thoroughbred owner we'd ever seen.

Word spread through the ranch that there was a new boy in town, and although every new horse gets attention, many people have an extra-soft spot for Thoroughbreds. The new guy had a flock of people at his stall when Debbie S. arrived, and she joined the hovering group out of curiosity. "I think we're going to call the new guy Jordan," Debbie S. heard someone say.

She walked past the admiring entourage and took a spot at the far rail, apart from the pack. To Debbie S.'s amazement, "Jordan" left the group and meandered over to her. Debbie S. reached in to greet him and he breathed into her wind, the natural way one horse greets another. Debbie S. replied in kind by blowing into him, which he inhaled, then gently laid his head down on her chest. The moment was an instant connection beyond any that Debbie S. had ever experienced in her many years working with horses.

"I have to have him," Debbie S. informed the group. Yes, this was the same woman who had sworn many times that she'd never adopt. She stepped into his stall to examine the rest of him and he nuzzled into her space. At 17.1 hands, he was huge and handsome. Absolutely perfect in Debbie S.'s eyes.

By the end of the day, Debbie S. had an announcement. "His name is Onyx, and he's mine!" She completed the adoption application that afternoon.

Like other Thoroughbreds, Onyx had spent his life confined to a stall for most of the day and rarely, if ever, socialized with either horses or humans. Debbie S. was thrilled to experience his joy at being released into the herd and running free among his kind.

We still tease her sometimes about adopting Onyx when she'd been so certain she never would. "That's before he stole my heart," she says.

Sometimes you just never know. Horses get into your blood and then there's no turning back.

CHAPTER 30

All of us in the legitimate rescue world have horses in our blood. Saving the animals is a goal we share, and generally, I see cooperation between different rescues for the sake of a horse. Then there are other times when I see competition among horse rescuers, similar to rival businesses in the corporate world. The competitive philosophy is bunk since there's no shortage of horses that need help, unfortunately. My approach has always been that the more of us there are working together to protect horses, the better. The principles of our C.L.E.A.R initiative guide us to extend help and support, both within our community and beyond.

Social media is the most significant instrument we use to spread our message to a broad audience. Its power is incredible and it's become our primary method of connecting with other horse rescue organizations and horse lovers in general. Our Facebook page administrator, Karen, manages the dialogue to and from the site.

In July 2014, we received the following message from Taylor Breen:[36]

"Hello, I'm trying to help out a little girl who loves horses and has cerebral palsy. Her name is Sam.[37] My goal is to mail her hundreds of drawings of horses. Please share my original post if possible. Thank you and I fully support what y'all do!"

Taylor had sought out horse-related organizations and forwarded his original post:

> Okay all my artist friends, I've got a simple request. One of my Facebook friends has a daughter named Sam. Sam has two favorite things in this world, one is getting regular mail, and the other is horses. Sam happens to have cerebral palsy, but she doesn't let that stop her from enjoying her life. She's had to overcome some great obstacles in her young life. So here's my request. I'll be drawing a picture or two of a horse and then mailing it to her. I'd love to be able to send as many drawings of horses as possible to her in that envelope. If you can find it in your heart sometime this week to draw a horse for her, sign it, then send me a digital copy of it so that I can print it and add it to the collection to be mailed to this very strong and very special little girl. It would make her day, and as artists, isn't that one of the most important things about the art that we create? If you are interested, please send me a Facebook message. I'd love for this thing to get huge. If I have to mail numerous envelopes full of drawings of horses, that would be awesome, so

---

[36] Name has been changed to protect privacy.
[37] Name has been changed to protect privacy.

please share this post as much as possible. Let's make a little girl's day y'all. Thanks.

Karen printed and posted the request in the RVR office for anyone interested to join the effort, and I forwarded it to our C.L.E.A.R educator. Debbie M. had proven to be a passionate ambassador in our community outreach efforts and this was potentially a good fit for her interests.

Sure enough, Debbie M. established contact with Taylor and learned that the response to his request for horse pictures had been so generous that he created another Facebook page dedicated solely for this purpose. With Sam's parents' blessing, "Sam Loves Horses"[38] had launched.

When Debbie M. perused the page, her heart melted as she learned more about Sam and the challenges she faced. The account read, "'Sam Loves Horses' is for a little girl named Sam. She loves horses and this page is where you can submit your horse drawings for her. (Samantha, or Sam as she prefers to be called, was born with cerebral palsy, but also is fighting heart problems, a seizure disorder, and has been in the hospital this summer with infections.)"

Debbie M. replied to the page that, although she isn't an artist, she has many pictures of the horses at RVR Horse Rescue. She offered to send photos and simple facts about horses to Sam. Her C.L.E.A.R educational material would be put to great use.

After Taylor assured Debbie M. that Sam likes anything to do with horses, Debbie M. hatched another plan. That afternoon, she would be leading a Critter Camp lesson at the Humane Society. Her presentation to the children would cover standard horse care and rescue. Maybe she could drum up some support for Sam at the same time?

---

[38] Name has been changed because this story is not being told to promote the family.

During her lesson, she explained the newly created "Sam Loves Horses" Facebook page and asked the children to draw pictures of horses for Sam. She assured them their efforts would brighten the girl's day. Many of the children immediately buried their heads in artwork, turning deaf ears to the remainder of Debbie M.'s presentation. She was touched by their bubbling excitement.

Once their finishing touches were complete, Debbie M. decided that a photo would be a sweet memento of this special outreach, but she lacked the parental permission she needed to photograph the children. Not one short on imagination, Debbie M. instructed her artists to cover their faces with their drawings. She then snapped a priceless memory of the twelve faceless munchkins.

Their gifts to Sam reflected innocence and compassion. Besides their spirited attempts at horse art, they reached out to their new virtual friend. One told Sam, "Hope you feel better, Sam. P.S. You are a very pretty girl and seem sweet. I have seen a picture of you!"

Debbie M. left Critter Camp with a full heart and twelve precious, original works of art. The next day, she prepared a package for Sam that included the children's drawings, a letter explaining who they were, and the photo she took of the class. When she referred to the Facebook page to get the mailing address, she was amazed to see that they'd racked up five hundred "likes" in only two days. The posts on the site conveyed Sam's excitement about her budding page and its rapidly growing popularity. The blond beauty was quickly stealing hearts across America.

Four days later, Debbie M. was touched to see a post of a beaming Sam displaying the photo of the anonymous Critter Camp children. The gap in her brilliant smile from two missing front teeth made an adorable girl even more endearing. Debbie M. was grateful that their efforts had made a difference.

Their common love of horses drew Debbie M. to Sam. She sent more photos and a note:

"My name is Debbie M. and I love horses, too. I love talking to kids about my two favorite subjects, dogs and horses. I have two rescued dogs now that live with my husband and me. I don't own any horses, but I'm lucky to be a volunteer at a horse rescue called RVR Horse Rescue. At RVR, there are always lots of horses needing love and attention. I like to take lots of photos of the horses at RVR, so I thought I would share a few with you."

In one of the enclosed photos, Shanti and Debbie M. were nose to nose. Her caption read: "I love this photo because Shanti is giving me horse kisses. She is over 20 years old and her feet were badly neglected in the past. It often hurts her to walk so she can't walk a long distance. Horses have big teeth and they can hurt you if they bite. Shanti was very gentle and we were both enjoying her wiggling her lips on my nose."

In another photo, Shanti stood in the shade of her stall, her head hanging low and eyes closed. Debbie M. wrote: "Horses can sleep lying down but only for an hour or two or they will start to have problems with their bodies. They take lots of short naps while standing up. In this photo, Shanti is taking a nap. She loves attention from people but was too tired to notice me. Poor sleepy Shanti!"

In another letter, she wrote: "I'm going to tell you about Destiny, one of RVR's horses whose feet were badly neglected. She is a seven-year-old palomino mare. Her owner left her in a field and never took care of her except giving her some food and water. The photo below is just one of her hooves when she came to RVR. All four hooves had been neglected. It has taken over six months of care from our farrier and lots of medicines to get her feet healthy again. The farrier uses tools like a rasp or file to rub off the rough edges and then he smoothes them further with a buffing tool. It doesn't hurt the horse, but they need to be taught to stand still so both the horse and farrier are safe."

The accompanying photos showed Destiny and her neglected "before" and healthy "after" hooves.

Debbie M. demonstrated the epitome of our C.L.E.A.R mission. Her latest student, Sam, was a young ailing stranger half a continent away. This was community outreach at its finest.

Since horse slaughter was banned in the United States, domestic slaughter has been reduced, but it was estimated that 146,548 horses were exported for slaughter in 2014.[39]

CHAPTER 31

All of our community outreach efforts are done to draw attention to our cause and stem the tide of abuse. One of the monumental challenges that contributes to the problem is the difficulty involved when rehoming a horse. Even euthanasia is an expensive proposition, costing a few hundred dollars. As a result, many horses are abandoned like a piece of trash or sent to slaughter, even though a federal ban prohibits the practice.

The world of slaughter is a dark secret hidden from mainstream Americans. It's a term that people have heard, but an easy one to ignore due to its gruesome nature. Although many horses are actually companion pets, they are legally considered livestock. With that designation, their protection under the law is precarious.

Backyard slaughterhouses remain prominent in cultural pockets around the country, where certain ethnic groups believe horse meat increases libido. Unscrupulous scammers peruse CraigsList for free or cheap horses and then send a woman and child to pick it up, giving the impression that the horse is going to a good home. Lo and behold, the animal will actually be butchered alive for its meat.

---

[39] Equine Welfare Alliance. "Mexican Horse Meat; The impact of the EU ban." www.equinewelfarealliance.org/uploads/Mexican_horse_meat_exports_analysis-FINAL.pdf (accessed 8/23/15).

When we are alerted about a case, we never know what we'll encounter. In one case, a neighbor sent a photograph showing a dark gangly baby hobbling down the road. His frail bony legs could barely support him, and one jetted out at an awkward angle as if he were a newborn giraffe trying to find his footing.

By the time we reached the location, neighbors had returned Tiny Tim and his mother, Angel, to their stall to ensure their safety until our arrival. The stall was piled with bodily waste, clearly indicating neglect. The water bucket held muddy green muck.

Angel's malnourishment prevented her from feeding her baby. They were both starving. In her desperation, Angel had broken free of their prison, freeing them both and allowing the Good Samaritan to spot her crippled son.

We replaced the muck with freshwater and waited for someone to come to the property. The first person to arrive was a man who denied the horses were his.

"They're the owners," he told us.

"Okay, but they're starving! Do you feed them?" I challenged, holding him accountable. My patience for apathetic witnesses is long gone.

"No, but the owner comes by every now and then," he reasoned. "He's going to eat them."

I had the man call the owner and tell him he had a choice. He could willingly give up the horses or I would call the sheriff's office and he would lose them to me anyway. Based on their deplorable condition, there was no doubt the authorities would confiscate them and put the owner on record. With that little twist of his arm, the man surrendered Angel and Tiny Tim to us.

Amazingly, Tiny Tim's leg wasn't broken and it straightened out quickly, allowing him to walk normally. As the pair became healthier and were eligible to be rehomed, a family fell in love with their Timmy and later adopted Angel, too.

We often threaten abusers with criminal charges, and doing so proved effective in the case of Tiny Tim and Angel, but the reality is that, between the wiggle room in the laws and other priorities of the judicial system, many cases are not prosecuted. We just keep our heads low and tackle as many as we can.

Angel and Tim's rescue at a backyard slaughterhouse involved fewer horses than a normal bust at a full-fledged slaughter facility. In those cases, there are generally more horses than any one rescue can handle. When that happens, we might be called upon to handle overflow from other areas of Florida, typically from the South Florida SPCA in Miami.

One case involved eight horses, two ponies, and a cow from an illegal slaughter farm in the east Everglades. The owner was charged with eleven counts each of animal cruelty and confinement of animals without food and water.

The man was drenched in blood when the officers arrived, insisting he had just slaughtered pigs for his consumption, but the horses on the property were emaciated and were fed nothing but the grass they could find.

Animal guts and carcasses were strewn around the gruesome scene. A severed cow head dripped blood onto terrified horses. Animals tied between trees were strung up and split open alive in front of the others. As long as there is demand for the meat, animals will continue to be killed.

In another case, we learned through Facebook that the SFSPCA needed to place twelve horses saved from slaughter. We agreed to take two Thoroughbred mares, River Rose and Flattering Irene. The day after their arrival we learned that River Rose had a three-year-old son, Fury, who had been delivered directly from the slaughterhouse to an adoptive home in Ocala.

After the separation from her son, Rose showed signs of distress. Her anxiety presented itself as cribbing, a typical compulsive behavior whereby the horse grabs a solid surface with its upper teeth and pulls backward while sucking in air. Our fence railings throughout the ranch show tattletale signs of this common vice, but Rose rocked and cribbed more than I've ever seen before. Tears streamed down her face. Her extreme stress would prevent Rose's recovery, so we needed to act quickly before she lost her will to live.

We decided to call the SPCA to see if Rose's son, Fury, was still available. They contacted Fury's adoptive parents and, once they explained Rose's circumstances, the family was happy to oblige and relinquish Fury to us.

We broadcasted our need for help with Fury's transportation and donations covered the cost to retrieve him. Our hope was that Rose would fight harder for her recovery with Fury at her side. Four volunteers picked up the boy and he was reunited with his mom that evening. The improvement in Rose was nearly immediate. She became calmer and showed more interest in food.

Fury lived up to his name in temperament, although Fabio would have been a more suitable name to describe his luxurious, flowing black mane. Having Fury by her side helped Rose, but her emotional recovery would be no easy feat. Only time would tell how far she could make it, but she filled our hearts with hope when she slowly began to emerge from her neurotic shell.

Fury, on the other hand, flew through his rehabilitation. We assumed the wild child would never be able to be ridden, but he proved us wrong. "He's fun to ride!" Sergio concluded after his evaluation. His approval led to a speedy adoption. Meanwhile, his presence had set Rose on the right path.

I'm not so naïve to think I can shut down the slaughter market, but we can make a difference to a few starfish. When I look into the eyes of a horse like Rose or Fury, I know each life is worth our effort.

The Henneke System was developed by Don R. Henneke, PhD, of Tarleton State University in Texas in 1983.[40]

CHAPTER 32

When I first started rescuing and saw firsthand the deplorable treatment of animals like Rose and Fury, an unstoppable warrior princess emerged from somewhere deep within me. In fact, the fighter who surfaced was simply my outrage at the horrors I was witnessing. Animals hovering on the verge of death at the hands of humans. The situations we encountered infuriated me. In my times of outrage, anyone who didn't know me would never believe I had a shy bone in my body.

Each rescue attempt has the propensity to turn hostile. Therefore, the most effective method to elicit cooperation is with a cool, calm head—but that just wasn't me.

One early morning phone call from a distraught woman alerted us to a horse who was lying on the ground behind a warehouse where she worked. The horse appeared to be dying and she wanted to know if there was anything that we could do.

We hooked up the trailer and arrived there within twenty minutes of her call. Thirty gawkers milled around the fallen skeleton on the ground. Saddle sores peppered Kimmie's back, indicating someone had been riding the emaciated mare, which was inexcusable in its own rite. On top of that, their improper techniques caused further damage, resulting in the painful sores. As if that wasn't enough torture, her shoes were hanging off,

---

[40] Robin Easley. "Body Condition Scores The Henneke System." August 22, 2009.
http://gerlltd.org/Education/Equine%20Body%20Condition%20Score%20Pr esentation.pdf (accessed 8/23/15).

confirming neglect of her overall care. Kimmie had been left in the field to die.

I blew a gasket. All the bystanders took a ration of my rage.

"WHO DID THIS?" I screamed at them, scanning the crowd. I knew someone must have witnessed something. Anger streamed down my face. I was cussing and ranting like a lunatic—totally derailed, I even chest-bumped a chosen few in my rampage to get information.

One man spoke up and said he saw a guy riding the Paso Fino mare on the road regularly. "Why didn't you do something about it then?" I challenged the poor sucker, nose to nose.

We finally got back to the business at hand and five of us lifted and guided Kimmie into the trailer. Her condition was extremely poor, but she could handle the short ride back to the ranch.

When we arrived at RVR, she proved to be the saddest, most defeated horse I had ever seen. Normally, when a new horse is introduced, they start hollering at the others. Not Kimmie. She exited the trailer with her head practically dragging on the ground. She couldn't care less about what was happening, an apathy that tore at the tear-soaked volunteers who were there to welcome her arrival.

Pete, the farrier, was on site and he removed her shoes as the first step of her recovery. In the meantime, I informed the sheriff's department so they could begin an investigation. Their evaluation placed Kimmie at a 0.5 on the Henneke Scale. This numeric tool was developed to quantify the body condition of a horse. The scale runs from a lower limit of one, which indicates extreme starvation, to ten, which indicates extreme obesity. Kimmie's pathetic condition was deemed worse than extreme starvation.

We placed our new girl into a segregated paddock during the intake process, as per usual. The quarantine allows us time to complete a medical examination, which includes Coggins testing, before releasing a potentially sick horse into the herd.

The Coggins test checks for equine infectious anemia, commonly called swamp fever. This disease is similar to HIV in humans and is transmitted by bloodsucking insects, primarily flies. Often the carriers don't display obvious symptoms, so every horse is quarantined until the testing is complete to prevent inadvertent transmission to healthy horses through bodily fluids.

Next was the hurdle of Kimmie's starvation. A bucket of food to a severely emaciated horse could literally kill it with kindness. If their emaciation has led to poor kidney or liver function, providing a lot of food can result in colic or shock or even death.

Oftentimes, horses deprived of food eat sand and dirt out of desperation. During their recovery, the foreign matter must be eliminated before their system can properly process real food again. As the sand or dirt passes, the animal will lose weight before gaining any, sometimes dropping up to thirty-five pounds worth of dirt.

The intake process includes dumping poop in a bucket of water to see how much sand precipitates out, and sometimes it's an enormous amount. Pitch-black poop can be an indicator of significant dirt.

Refeeding begins with tiny amounts of mushy high-protein alfalfa hay or pellets about six times a day. The amount is gradually increased and grains are added, along with a small amount of dry alfalfa hay. If we see signs of distress, we stop adding. As the amount of food per feeding increases, the number of feedings per day is reduced until the patient is eating normal-size meals two or three times per day.

Our regimen acclimates the body to food again. Initially, it seems as though you're not feeding them anything, but it's all they can handle. We fine-tuned our process over time and out of necessity. Our veterinarians couldn't provide much guidance in this area because people who starve their animals don't typically provide them with medical care.

We immediately started Kimmie on her refeeding regimen and the skeletal mare gradually gained weight. She returned to good health and was introduced into the herd. She'll play out the rest of her days at RVR Horse Rescue, grazing in the pasture with her buddy, Freddy. She'll never have to worry about when her next meal will come, but she still knocks on her stall at feeding time to remind her caregivers that she's waiting.

Kimmie is one example of why we try so hard and spend money on animals who are teetering at death's door. Because you never know. Many horses that I thought would never survive, end up thriving. That's exactly what we're about: giving a second chance.

The day of Kimmie's rescue was a turning point for me. Based on my extreme reaction, I decided that I could no longer retrieve the horses. It requires someone calmer and more collected than I had been. My blow-up had been detrimental to the situation as well as to my health. Something had to change and I was ready to hand over the reins.

I approached Debbie S. about becoming the chairperson for rescue retrieval. She had impressed me with her cool head and savvy manipulation of the man who was reluctant to let us help the dying baby with the cow collar.

"I like how you handled Angel's rescue," I said. "We were all hyper, telling the owner he was going to jail, but you stayed calm."

With Debbie S.'s consent, I presented my proposal to the board and they approved. While each retrieval stole a little piece of my soul, Debbie S. found it to be rewarding, proving she was a perfect fit.

The actual removal of a horse is often confrontational and tragic. We've heard every lie and excuse in the book. People become defensive and angry, and the condition of the horses is generally heart wrenching. But Debbie S. still finds it extremely satisfying because the horses seem to know we are there to save them.

When we arrive, their typical reaction seems to convey a clear message: *I don't know where that trailer's going, but I'm getting on it.* The case of Mr. Black and Miss White was a perfect example. The pair of horses wandered onto a beautiful, expansive cattle farm. The rancher allowed them to stay on his seventy-five acres for about a year, although they only had grass to eat. Finally, he decided they should be somewhere where they'd have proper food and care, which was when he called us.

When Debbie S. arrived, she and the rancher went in search of the horses, who might have been anywhere on the sprawling property. "Hopefully they will be close by," the man said and then they spotted Black and White in the front pasture. The rancher planned to fill a bucket of grain to entice them, while Debbie S. walked into field. Sure enough, both horses approached her.

The guy was stunned. "Huh? I've never seen *that* before," he muttered. "They must know you're here for them."

Miss White followed Debbie S. to the trailer and loaded in like a dream. Boom. "I'm ready to go!" she seemed to say. She then turned back to face her buddy. "Hurry up . . . you getting on?" Her look summoned Mr. Black.

Boom. Mr. Black loaded.

The man stood dumbfounded. "Do they know?" he asked Debbie S.

Yes, they know.

CHAPTER 33

The rescue of Mr. Black and Miss White was easy compared to most. Horse rescue is generally not a job for the faint-hearted and not something many people would willingly undertake. Every once in a while we experience an unlikely hero who contributes to our mission with incredible spirit, compassion, and grit.

Juan[42] happens to be one of those special people who has gone down in our record books as perfectly demonstrating our C.L.E.A.R principles. The young man had become familiar with horses from time spent on his family's Paso Fino horse farm in Puerto Rico, where Juan's father still lived. The specialized show horse breed prances with a smooth, delicate four-beat gait, similar to the Tennessee Walker.

As a broke teenager, Juan didn't have the means to purchase a horse, but that fact didn't dampen his desire to own one. A friend who knew he was looking for a free animal called Juan about a possible lead and he rushed over.

Upon his arrival at the property, he was drawn to commotion around back. He approached the tense and frenzied group hovering over a bloody body, poised to shoot. The bay mare with a tiny star marking on her forehead had apparently been tied up to a tree when she spooked and broke free of the rope. In her hysteria, she became entangled in barbed wire. The

---

[41] RVR Horse Rescue's Facebook page. https://www.facebook.com/RVRHorseRescue (accessed 8/22/15).
[42] Name has been changed to protect privacy.

talons had sliced her legs and damaged a hoof. She was beyond help and they were going to put her down. Juan was terrified, but plunged into the action.

"Don't shoot her!" he shouted. "I'm going to take care of her!"

"You can't," they told him.

"YES! Don't shoot her!" he cried, now also petrified that he was defying armed men intent on killing. He pushed the horse's head away and stood between the man and the mare.

They scoffed at the naïve man-child as he proceeded to collect pieces of twine off the ground that had been used to secure hay bales. The twine became a make-shift rope that he would use to lead the horse away from her certain death.

Desperate, Juan called his brother-in-law, who hitched up the trailer and drove to the boy's aid, along with Juan's sister and mother. Unfortunately, a flat tire on the trailer prevented them from loading the victim until a repair was made.

Juan's brother-in-law helped calm the agitated gunman. He emptied the chamber of bullets to restore safety to the scene. Handing over the $50 he had in his pocket, Juan's brother-in-law asked the man to leave the horse unharmed until they could pick her up the next day, which he did.

Uncertain where he would take his new horse, Juan was short on options, but his brother-in-law once again came to his aid. Juan could keep the horse on his rental property. There was no shelter or fence, but it was a start.

Juan's immediate priority was tending to the medical needs of his mare, named Mona Lisa. In the following days, he built a makeshift two-stall stable with pallets he'd acquired from Home Depot and covered it with a tarp. The surrounding fence, which he'd also created using pallets, provided a turnout area for grazing. Overwhelmed by his enormous undertaking, he found extra hours by skipping school.

Unable to afford veterinary care, but well beyond his own expertise, Juan consulted his father in Puerto Rico, as well as local vets for advice on how to treat Mona Lisa's wounds. He applied Biozine gel and Wonder Dust to her gaping sores and administered a tetanus shot, per the vet's recommendation. As the weeks wore on, Juan hustled at odd jobs for Mona Lisa's food and medical treatment expenses.

The woman who lived on the property watched the story play out in amazement. The boy arrived every morning and evening to feed, water, and care for his horse. They'd lay together in the shade of a tree, sometimes napping. His actions proclaimed a deep love.

But as the weeks wore on, Juan found himself in trouble both at school and home, and he felt increasing pressure to get rid of Mona Lisa. The family was struggling to pay for her food and medical needs, even foregoing a necessary car repair to care for the horse. Juan had slipped in over his head. For six weeks, the fifteen-year-old boy had moved mountains to care for the injured mare, but his time had run out.

He began his search to rehome Mona Lisa by Googling "help for horses." That search term led him to horse rescue sites and he started making phone calls but his pleas came up empty. One place wouldn't take her and another was full. His desperate next attempt was RVR.

The photos Juan sent us of the bloody but gorgeous Thoroughbred were more than enough to justify the rescue. Debbie S. was on it. When she spoke with the teen to gather more details, his love and compassion poured out in his broken English.

"What's her name?" Debbie S. asked him.

"It's Mona Lisa, because she's beautiful," he answered. "You'll see how beautiful she is."

After he gave the abbreviated background information, Debbie S. assured him we would pick up Mona Lisa that day and help her.

"If you don't mind, I'm not sure if I can be there to see her go," he said with emotion crackling his words, "but the lady who lives on the property will open the gate for you. I've seen your Facebook page and I know you'll take good care of her." Affection laced his Spanish accent. "She's going to be amazing."

"It's fine if you don't want to be there, but will you leave me a note saying you're the owner of the horse and that you give RVR permission to take her?" Debbie S. requested. We can't legally remove an animal without the owner's permission.

"Yes, ma'am," Juan assured her.

When Debbie S. arrived on site, she was thoroughly impressed with the living quarters Juan had built for Mona Lisa and another horse he had recently rescued.

The pictures Debbie S. had seen told a terrible story, but seeing the damage in person was even more shocking. The oozing open gashes poured trails of blood down her legs. Juan's medication on the wounds was obvious.

Debbie S. slowly led Mona Lisa to the trailer. In addition to the raw wounds on her legs, one of her hooves was damaged. Debbie S. allowed her as much time as she needed, as Mona Lisa was undeniably hurting. Once they got to the trailer, she was cooperative to load, but stepping up to enter hurt her injured hoof and legs, causing her to hesitate.

Juan arrived unexpectedly before they left, and when Mona Lisa saw him, she gingerly backed off the trailer. Each of her movements was as painful as when she'd loaded, but she was determined to see the young man she'd grown to love. When she reached Juan, she gently laid her head on his shoulder.

He spoke to her sweetly. "Mona, these people are going to take care of you. I've done all I can do. You have to get better, so you have to get on the trailer." Juan then gathered a bucket of feed to coax her back inside.

"She's a good girl. She's really a good girl," he kept insisting to Debbie S. "I'll get her on the trailer. I promise she's a good girl." Perhaps he was nervous that Debbie S. might be having second thoughts, but she wasn't going anywhere without that horse.

Realizing Mona Lisa's pain, Juan rinsed her wounds with bottled water he was carrying. "If you do this first, and let it soften a little bit, it will help the pain and make it better to step on the trailer." He instructed Debbie S., who was touched by his kindness and gentleness.

Shortly thereafter, Juan walked onto the trailer, leading his girl. Once she was loaded, he stepped out the side door. She peered at him through the window and released a pitiful whinny.

"Aren't you coming with me?" she seemed to ask him.

He said good-bye to her, but he still wasn't ready himself. He reentered the trailer and plopped down on the floor. Mona Lisa bent down to nestle her head in his lap. The tight-knit bond between them was undeniable.

Debbie S. heard the one-way Spanish conversation taking place inside the trailer, but she didn't understand the words. When Juan exited, she asked him what he told Mona.

"I told her she saved my life, too," he stated. "I said I hope she helps somebody, and that she's a good girl. Maybe I can come see her?" he asked Debbie S., and of course she welcomed him with open arms. "I'm going to save my money and come see her," he promised.

When Mona Lisa arrived at RVR and was evaluated by our vet, he surmised that her wounds hadn't been inflicted by barbed wire, as Juan had been told, but by ropes tied to her legs to drag her. It was his supposition based on how symmetrical the wounds had been. It wasn't the first and wouldn't be the last time that we may not have gotten the real or full story of the torture our horses had encountered. In any case, the vet was impressed with the care Juan had provided.

"He saved her life," the vet told us. "It's good he did what he did when he did it."

The Ian Somerhalder Foundation,[43] a nonprofit organization that aims to positively impact the planet and its creatures, supported Mona Lisa's costly rehabilitation. Her treatment required ongoing scraping, medicating, and wrapping of her overgrown proud flesh wounds. The pulpy growths stemmed from the wide gashes, and she tolerated their removal and any other procedures perfectly. She knew she was being helped.

We anticipated long-term nerve damage to her legs, but Mona Lisa healed completely. Within two months of her arrival, she had acclimated to the herd and her frisky, friendly personality had blossomed. Watching her frolic and chase and sprint with her paddock mates was all the proof we needed that Mona Lisa would be just fine. Her progress thrilled all of her loyal Facebook cheerleaders.

Debbie S. sent pictures depicting Mona Lisa's progress to Juan, who still hadn't been able to visit his girl.

"I told you she would be good," he reminded Debbie S. "I promised her she would run one day."

[43] Ian Somehalder Foundation. "About the IS Foundation." www.isfoundation.com/about-foundation (accessed 8/23/15).

In today's world, children with cerebral palsy often benefit from several traditional treatments and therapies designed to greatly enhance his or her abilities. Some therapies [. . .] like equine therapy—also known as hippotherapy—take an unconventional path in the effort to increase a child's physical strength and cognitive capabilities.[44]

CHAPTER 34

We all love a happy ending like Mona Lisa's. We see so much cruelty in the rescue business that each victory becomes a sweet sugar nugget in a bitter, stale cup of coffee. The story of Taylor and his little Sam was another sweet nugget, and we enjoyed watching the story continue to play out.

Taylor Breen was a Good Samaritan on a mission to rally his friends and strangers to draw horses for Miss Sam, whom he didn't even know. His simple drawing project had mushroomed and then taken an unexpected turn.

Six days after his initial request for horse drawings, Taylor made another post. This time he included a link to a popular fund-raising site. He wrote:

> Hello Everyone,
>
> Sam, a seven-year-old little girl and her horse, PeanutButterCup, are about to restore your faith in humanity.
>
> Let me introduce you to Sam and PeanutButterCup. Sam is a very special girl whose smile could brighten the darkest day. She

---

[44] MyChild. "Hippotherapy." http://cerebralpalsy.org/about-cerebral-palsy/treatment/therapy/hippotherapy/# (accessed 8/23/15).

is a child who, once you meet her, you will never forget. She also happens to have cerebral palsy. Sam cannot walk without the aid of a walker or assistance. She has already been through more than most adults have in her short life thus far. Yet she has the strength to smile and fight through it all. Little Sam has changed my life forever . . . and I've only known her for nine days.

My name is Taylor and nine days ago I was contacted by Sam's mother, Walinda,[45] and she asked me if I would draw a horse for her little girl who has cerebral palsy. See, Sam loves getting regular mail and she absolutely loves horses. Horses are especially helpful for kids who have cerebral palsy because riding a horse helps strengthen certain muscles and relax others. Miss Sam loves to ride horses. So, being an artist, I agreed, and then I got to thinking . . . What if I could get my other artist friends to draw some horses for Sam as well and then mail them to her? After a few Facebook posts in a single day, the list of people wanting to draw little Sam a horse became a lot bigger than I'd previously imagined it would. Sam's parents were very happy to hear about this.

So I started thinking again . . . What if I could make a Facebook page just for Sam, where everybody could post their horse artwork online for her parents to show her. So, with her mother's permission, I did so and the Facebook page "Sam Loves Horses" was born. That was last Tuesday.

---

[45] Name has been changed to protect privacy.

The page instantly started gaining attention and passed 100 "likes" on the first day. People started posting not only drawings for little Sam but also photos. Everybody started writing encouraging and supportive words for both Sam and her family. The page kept getting bigger by the day.

It's now Monday morning, 3:25 a.m., six days after the page began. The page hasn't slowed down and now has 733 page "likes." The amount of beautiful artwork, photos, and posts that everyone is posting for Sam on a daily basis has become almost too hard for her parents and me to keep up with and we couldn't be happier about that. Every morning Sam's mom and her husband Willie[46] show Sam all the beautiful messages, drawings, and photos on the page. In Sam's own words, this was her response: "All this for little ol' me?"

Now if that wasn't amazing enough, my fiancée had originally suggested that maybe we could start a fund-raiser to get her a horse. I spoke with Sam's parents and they said it would be a wonderful thing to happen. They already had a place for a horse for Sam (one of Sam's nurses has a stable ten minutes away from Sam's house), so we started looking into how much a horse would cost, etc. Then, Saturday morning I was contacted by a loving and generous woman named Marianne[47] who wanted to give Sam one of her amazing horses named PeanutButterCup. Marianne was going to be moving soon but could

---

[46] Name has been changed to protect privacy.
[47] Name has been changed to protect privacy.

hold onto PeanutButterCup until the 15th of August for us.

Now PeanutButterCup isn't just an ordinary horse. PeanutButterCup is a horse that started out with a very rough life, then was rescued by the family of a little girl. That little girl helped PeanutButterCup recover and he grew to love her. When the girl grew up, she gave PeanutButterCup to Marianne.

Marianne teaches horseback riding and she knew that PeanutButterCup would love to be around children again. PeanutButterCup has also had previous experience with children who have cerebral palsy. He is an extremely beautiful, loving, and caring horse who really needs another special little girl to care for him and love him in return.

Now for the reason we need this fundraiser . . .

PeanutButterCup lives in Florida, and Sam and her family live in Wyoming.[48] Because PeanutButterCup is the perfect special horse for a little girl with cerebral palsy, we need to get that horse to her.

Since day one, when Sam's mother asked me to draw a horse for her daughter, everything has seemed to lead up to a special moment. Now I am certain that it was for this very moment. This destiny for a little girl and a horse.

The money from this fund-raiser will be used for the safe transportation of

---

[48] State has been changed to protect privacy.

PeanutButterCup from Florida to Wyoming, feed for the horse for at least a year, any veterinary costs that will need to be covered or that may arise, grooming, maintenance of the horses hooves, and for the horse's lodging. This fund-raiser initially needs to at least cover the cost of transporting PeanutButterCup, which will be between one and two thousand dollars by the 7th or 8th of August. . . .

In order for those funds to be raised, this project for Sam and this fund-raiser need to go viral. Please tweet about it, post it on Facebook and share it, and tell all of your friends and family.

If everyone that reads this could donate at least a dollar, and then share it on their Facebook page, then this deadline and goal can be reached. If you cannot donate, which . . . I completely understand, then please share this fund-raiser page. This cannot happen without everyone's help. Once the transportation for PeanutButterCup is paid for and taken care of, this page will continue to accept donations for the ongoing and future care of PeanutButterCup.[49]

This project started as a gift to Sam and her family and I would like to make sure that they are not burdened by this gift in any way, so any funds left over will be used for the care of the horse and any expenses for Sam.

Every little girl deserves a horse, but in my humble opinion, especially our Sam. Please help us make a little girl's life a bit brighter, just

---

[49] Fund-raiser is no longer active and this story is not an advertisement or promotion for the family.

because you can. Thank you from the bottom of my heart.

Taylor - Semper Fi.

Taylor and his fiancée had since met with Marianne and PeanutButterCup to ensure the offer was legitimate and the horse was sound before launching the campaign. The Marine veteran had never seen this turn of events coming, even two weeks prior.

*Romeo is our Miracle Boy, the poster child
for our mission, and the crowd favorite of our
Facebook followers.*

CHAPTER 35

Taylor was right to ensure Sam's family was not unduly burdened by the gift of PeanutButterCup. Horse care of any kind is costly, but care of sickly rescue horses is even more expensive. Treating neglected hooves and floating teeth and providing vaccinations on top of other existing medical needs racks up a steep tab quickly. If the rescued horse shows a will to live, we do whatever we can to help them. We have to try. I can predict which ones will pull through and which ones won't, but I'm not correct 100 percent of the time. Therefore, whenever a horse is willing to fight, we join them in battle.

One day a Good Samaritan called us for advice about a horse they had rescued out of someone's backyard. The owner tied up Romeo on his property before he left for his prison sentence. The jerk had also attempted a backyard castration on the gray stallion, resulting in a botched job.

A neighbor girl took Romeo under her wing, providing water and scraps of food on the owner's property until she convinced her family to bring him home. However, their good intentions couldn't compensate for their lack of horse knowledge and they were quickly overwhelmed.

The caller said Romeo was very sick with diarrhea and they were looking for suggestions on how to feed him. As the conversation continued, it became apparent that Romeo was far worse than the inexperienced neighbors could handle and we asked them to send us some pictures of the sick boy.

The photos were revolting and told the true story that the caller hadn't been able to articulate. It was so bad that we had to step in. I assumed he wouldn't make it, but we would try.

He was a 0.5 on the Henneke scale and I had no idea how he was still alive. He had no functioning bowel, only pus oozed out of his backside. The loss of muscle memory from his emaciated state caused his rectum to droop open a full three inches, enough to reach in and touch his intestines. Bumps on his jaws indicated another issue, although we were unsure of their cause. Inside and out, infections decimated the skin and bones he had become. His condition was despicable and his body was shutting down.

Once we had him back at the ranch, we realized there was simply no way to keep the infection out. The situation appeared hopeless.

Dr. Gold determined that his facial bumps were the result of bad teeth, which we later had removed. One of his testes had retracted, a condition known as cryptorchid. Medicated baths, hydrotherapy, and around-the-clock care were the doctor's orders.

In addition to his medical treatment, we began the standard refeeding regimen.

Between his Wheaties and the medical treatment, he slowly stepped back from the brink. His butt started closing. He was fighting to survive, pleasing us all.

Three weeks later his testes dropped and we were able to castrate him properly. It became clear he was on the road to recovery, which I really never expected, based on his original atrocious condition. Usually when they're hovering at the precipice, like Romeo had been, their organs shut down and we lose them.

Romeo was still recuperating when Dawn attended an Awareness Day event at RVR for the first time. The gray gelding was quarantined in the round pen near the office, and his pathetic, sad appearance grabbed her attention. She had never seen a horse so skinny, and she'd been around horses all her life. Romeo convinced her to become a volunteer that day.

There was a fund-raiser being planned that would take place at Joia's, a local pizza and martini bar. We would have show-and-tell horses on hand to drum up more publicity for the cause, and Romeo had been selected to represent our mission.

Due to Dawn's extensive experience with horses, Sandy suggested that our newbie volunteer prepare Romeo for the Joia's event. The shy and serious half-pint befriended the recovering Romeo. She began by bathing and brushing him. They walked around the paddock and around the property. Their friendship blossomed and his trust in her followed.

One day Dawn started running on the outside of his paddock and he ran with her, following along on the inside. Later, when she called his name from across the yard and he whinnied back in reply, he sealed the deal. She was officially smitten.

When Dawn began volunteering, she'd sworn to herself that she wasn't going to adopt a horse. She had owned them previously and wasn't looking for another one, but she wanted to support a good cause by helping at the ranch.

Her love of horses had originated in her childhood in New York. At age eight, she convinced her divorced mom to send her away to a summer camp to learn how to ride a horse—and she was hooked. Although Dawn's mother was inexperienced when it came to horses, she wanted to support her daughter's interest and bought Dawn her first horse when she was twelve years old.

Dawn rode every weekend, thanks to the generosity of her grandmother. To pay for her riding, Dawn contributed half the cost by dipping into her lunch money while her grandmother provided the other half. This arrangement earned her one hour of riding each week.

As she grew, so did her love of horses. When she later married and had children, horses remained a part of their lives. But there was something extra special about Romeo. He seemed to be pulling out the pieces of shrapnel that had embedded in her soul after her son Shane's untimely and tragic passing, followed shortly thereafter by her beloved mother. Dawn's world had crumbled.

But now that she'd established a relationship with Romeo, Dawn noticed him perking up. His once-sunken form plumped with fat and muscle, restoring both body and spirit. She kept her eye on him, but reminded herself the timing wasn't right to adopt him, or any horse.

Dawn was nursing her ailing dog, who had begun having seizures. Old Moto needed Dawn's time and attention and she was committed to seeing him through. Not one to shirk responsibility, she told herself she wouldn't adopt Romeo until she could give him the attention he deserved and needed. She would pamper her dog for his remaining days and take the chance that Romeo might be adopted in the meantime. If she and Romeo were meant to be together, they would.

About four months later, Moto passed away and Romeo was still waiting for her. Now Dawn was ready. Romeo's adoption was finalized shortly thereafter, before Dawn even knew whether he was rideable or not. She loved and wanted him regardless. If she couldn't ride him, he'd make a good pet. Yes, a huge pet, but a good one nevertheless.

The day of the adoption, Dawn's excitement overflowed. She jumped on Romeo for the first time, bareback with his halter, and rode him around the pen. He was perfect. *What was I thinking?* she wondered in hindsight, but they shared such chemistry that she didn't doubt his reaction to her would be anything but sweet.

Eight short months after his rescue, the pathetic emaciated skeleton had transformed into a majestic, muscular beauty, exceeding everyone's expectations. Thankfully, Romeo proved me wrong and he became the poster child for what our rescue represents. He's our Miracle Boy.

Once his body was restored, his fiery spirit was also. He's a Casanova with the ladies, but a bully with the other geldings, which earned him his own harem of mares in their dedicated pasture.

As for Dawn, the mere mention of Romeo's name triggers a megawatt smile that crinkles her eyes. She visits him daily and he cheers her up without fail. They've incorporated trail riding into their routine, in addition to their walks. Each interaction strengthens their already solid bond.

In mom-like fashion, Dawn spoils her baby. He's been to hell and back, so he gets whatever he wants, enjoying the life of a prima donna. The big lug rummages her pockets for the cookies he knows will be there. Dawn's money, no longer needed for her grown human children, is now diverted to her equine child.

She marvels at how the whole process evolved. "So many people prayed for him and I guess it worked. He has come such a long way. I couldn't ask for a better horse."

Dawn and Romeo have a beautiful love story with a happy ending. He lights her up like a giddy schoolgirl, hiding any trace of her once-shattered heart. "I didn't adopt him," she says, reflecting on their journey. "He adopted me."

The symptoms for any form of colic are clear.
A horse will indicate it is in pain, and the
onset is often sudden [. . .] It will sweat, paw
at the ground, purse its lips, kick out, perhaps
try to bite its stomach region. They may roll,
perhaps assuming unusual positions in doing
so. [. . .]
If the cause is a twisted bowel, the prognosis
is poor unless the horse is well enough to
undergo urgent abdominal surgery.[50]

CHAPTER 36

Romeo is our fan-favorite rescue to date and Dawn is one of my many reliable volunteers. It's with the tremendous support of my Rescue Angels, like Dawn, that I've been able to grow the ranch beyond my wildest dreams.

So much has changed from that day long ago when we drove up to a property that brought my mother to tears. Although surrounding housing developments threaten to encroach our borders, the increasing bustle and congestion on six-lane Highway 301 quickly fades away for the remaining few miles leading to the ranch. The final stretch ends in rutted dirt at the gated entrance.

Majestic southern live oak trees drip with Spanish moss and provide a light reprieve from the relentless Florida sun. Their branches reach horizontally before winding and twisting their way to the brilliant sky above.

A handcrafted RVR sign adorns the chain-link gate that is locked across the driveway from evening until morning, when

---

[50] Horsetalk. "Coping with Colic." November 25, 2012.
http://horsetalk.co.nz/2012/11/25/coping-with-colic/#axzz3jfGQWZzN
(accessed 8/23/15).

it is opened for the arriving volunteers. Cars trickle into the parking area outside the gate. Signs attached to the wooden fence posts discourage well-intended visitors bearing treats: "Please do not feed the horses . . ."

Inside the gates the driveway splits two pastures and ends with a circular loop at the hub of the property, in front of my house. A chain-link fence around the house and yard contains Max, who performs his border patrol of the enclosure faithfully. The charming brown house with a complete wraparound porch is worn. Its upkeep has been for necessity rather than for appearance. My home is functional and simple, just the way I want it. Its strategic position gives me views of the surrounding land and the pond that separates my backyard from the outlying pasture.

The office we built years ago sits just across a cart path from my front yard. Essentially an oversized shed, the office is the brains of the operation. It contains desks, computers, refrigerator, a movie theater–popcorn machine, a variety of miscellaneous horse stuff, and clutter from a barrage of volunteers throughout the day and evening. Workers congregate at a table outside the office to enjoy some camaraderie and perhaps a cigarette or two. At the beginning of a shift, responsibilities are divvied up using the "divide and conquer" method, and then the group scatters.

Continuing clockwise around the hub, the hanging bench swing sways in the breeze near the fire pit that sometimes still smolders in the morning after a long, lazy evening of fellowship. Multiple pastures surround the hub. One just beyond the break area and adjacent to the office is the round pen used as the quarantine area for new or sickly residents, due to its high level of visibility. Its location is perfect for constant surveillance for any indications of a problem.

Five other pastures encircle the hub, although portable gates partition off additional sections as needed. The pond behind my house divides the front of the property from the back, where the expansive pasture is reserved for the bordered rehabilitated rescues.

Each day unfolds to the same routine, under the watchful eye of Sandy six days of the week, and I cover Sunday. The first feeding begins at about nine o'clock. The point person, who leads the volunteers of the particular shift, carefully portions the meals. The horse name and dietary recipe is communicated on a sticker attached to each feed bucket, a method that ensures no mistakes are made with ever-revolving hands.

The horses are fed in their stalls to prevent fighting and to ensure each one gets the proper food and amount. When all the horses of a particular pasture are finished eating, the group is turned back out for the remainder of the day, until the next feeding, which normally occurs two or three times per day.

Volunteers muck the stalls and paddocks. Fresh manure is added to the compost pile that ultimately fertilizes the pastures. Water buckets are cleaned and refilled or topped with freshwater. Chunky brown mineral blocks in milk crates, like giant lollipops, provide a licking pleasure and additional nutrients.

Hay is dropped into each pasture and might be soaked in water to soften and/or drain the sugar first, depending on the dietary needs of a given animal. Healthier horses get standard Tifton hay, which has low nutritional content, but keeps them full and busy. Those in recovery are fed the more nutritional and costly alfalfa hay.

Under normal circumstances, the horses are only stalled for feeding. As herd animals, they enjoy the companionship of the others, even sleeping together. Horses occasionally sleep standing up, especially while napping during the day, but generally lie down at night. In a typical herd, one stands guard while the others sleep. Having the donkeys as part of the herd increases the safety of the horses, because they're natural fighters and ward off predators who might sneak in for an attack.

The various pastures allow us to create herds based on personality types and knowing which animals get along with each other. Normally the ranch is peaceful and serene, with only the occasional whinny or snort or stampeding during play time. The most regular ruckus is caused by the impatient and hungry horses reminding the volunteers that it's feeding time with loud and insistent knocking on the stalls.

But horses can get mean and aggressive, as proven by the holes kicked in the stall walls. Therefore, creating a harmonious herd dynamic is critical. It's a constant juggling act choosing which horses are placed together. Each time a new horse comes out of quarantine, and every time a horse is adopted, it means a new herd is created.

I watch and come to know the different personalities, and I typically find the right combinations, but sometimes Mother Nature hands me the answer. For example, Mr. Black and Luna formed a friendship across the fence before they were moved into the same pasture. And Charity made no bones about her love of donkeys, when she confiscated Dominick as soon as he joined us and then continued to adopt each new donkey upon its arrival.

Sometimes reorganizing the herds is more of a challenge. Dawn's boy, Romeo, ended up segregated with his harem of mares after butting heads with every gelding he encountered.

One day after we reorganized the herds, including the donkeys, the changes seemed to be met with approval. After a tireless day of tending to tasks, the few of us remaining diehards enjoyed the mesmerizing yellow and red streaks dancing and licking at the air in the fire pit. Friendship and magical fairy dust blanketed our group until about eleven o'clock when Cowboy started raising Cain about Stella. His bellows shattered the peaceful silence and we sprung to our feet. The normally docile giant was pitching a fit and an all-out brawl seemed imminent. "Get this old biddy out of here," he seemed to demand, and we dashed to Stella's aid.

When we moved Stella into the adjacent pen, we discovered Mona Lisa lying down. Again. She had been in the same spot earlier that day. Not only does lying down for long periods cause troublesome pressure on intestines and internal organs, it can indicate a problem as well.

A horse resting on the ground during hot and muggy weather isn't that unusual, but the day had been cool and overcast, so something wasn't quite right. Additionally, Mona Lisa had acted out uncharacteristically during the medical treatment of her legs. We needed to keep an eye on her.

Not only was Mona Lisa on the ground again, but she was rolling and looking at her belly, a telltale sign of potentially fatal colic. We started walking her to keep her up and moving, hoping to resolve whatever troubled her gut. What had started out as drama for Stella quickly switched to a crisis for Mona Lisa.

We walked and ran her, taking turns, praying and willing her innards to correct themselves. However, instead of improving, her condition continued to deteriorate and she became more determined to get to the ground.

With heavy heart, I called Brandon Equine. I was destroyed. I could not afford the $12,000 it would cost to perform the surgery to try to save her.

While waiting for the vet to arrive, Mona's complete desperation unleashed. She literally threw herself on the golf cart, dropped herself near the smoldering fire, frantically buckling under to get to the ground.

"Stop!" I said. "Leave her alone and let her roll. The vet is on the way."

The poor girl had come to RVR after escaping an imminent death only by the sheer courage and grit of young Juan, undergone frequent and painful treatments to her proud flesh wounds, only to die of a twisted gut? It was heartbreaking.

Left to her own devices, Mona threw herself to the ground, first on one side, then onto the other. She rolled and groaned in horrific pain.

Then, as if a switch had been flipped, she suddenly sat up. When she remained still, I realized she had untwisted.

"She's alright," I announced to the others. Calm fell over our tattered group and we breathed easily for the first time since Cowboy threw his conniption fit.

The frantic mare had slipped back to her typical calm demeanor. We offered her molasses water for the additional sugars and nutrients, like we use during the cooler winter months to supplement the regular water. Mona Lisa pawed and played in the water bucket. She lapped up the sweet liquid goodness as if she couldn't get enough. The mare who had been throwing herself to the ground in pain just seconds before was playing like a baby.

The vet arrived and examined Mona Lisa. Her heart rate was elevated but decreasing. "Are you *sure* this horse was twisted?" he asked.

"Most definitely, yes!" we assured him.

He knew they were likely coming out to put her down, but she was fine now. "Y'all got lucky," he said, but we already knew that.

I believed we had just witnessed a miracle.

Natural horsemanship, colloquially known as horse whispering, is a collective term for a variety of horse-training techniques that have seen rapid growth in popularity since the 1980s.[51]

CHAPTER 37

When Cowboy and Stella got into their spat, they potentially saved Mona Lisa by allowing us to discover her condition. Their tiff also underscored the necessity for getting the herd dynamic right. Each animal species has biological forces that establish how the animals interact with one another. The horse world is no exception.

A hierarchical structure organizes the herd. Dominant players run the show and the remaining pecking order flows down from the top. Pinning back of the ears is the universal warning for "give me space or you will get hurt." It's a silent yet powerful communication.

In a relationship between a horse and a human, the human must establish himself as the leader or else the relationship is likely to be riddled with struggles. Sending improper or conflicting signals to a horse can also confuse him, leading to frustration for both the horse and human. Even if the horse is trying to please the owner, he may not understand what he's being asked to do. Clear communication and leadership beget obedience.

In the equine world, just as in the human world, there are varying schools of thought on the best or most effective techniques to instill submission. Breaking a horse, otherwise

---

[51] Wikipedia. "Natural horsemanship." https://en.wikipedia.org/wiki/Natural_horsemanship (accessed 8/23/15).

known as obedience training, is traditionally based on dominance or fear. In more recent years, several methods that focus on "natural horsemanship" have gained traction. I insist that Sergio use a rainbows-and-butterflies approach with our horses, but many of our adoptive families uphold the philosophy of a softer approach. Although the techniques differ, their principles all involve a humane and natural rapport with horses, similar to the communication between free-roaming animals.

One such method is the Parelli Natural Horsemanship method. This practice focuses on instinctual equine behaviors and builds the relationship between horse and rider on trust and respect, yet it establishes the human as the leader.

Marc Kaufman is a local trainer specializing in the Parelli technique. His reputation extends deep into the horse community at large and we've come to know him through his work with our adoptive families and their horses.

One of Marc's students, Cynthia, was a novice horsewoman when she first began lessons with Marc. What she lacked in experience, she made up for in passion. The term "animal lover" doesn't quite do Cynthia justice. Her twelve dogs, two parrots, and three cats, including one fluffy, tiny, adorable Russian Blue stray kitten she bottle-fed, makes her a tad more extreme than a typical animal lover.

Besides furry creatures, another of Cynthia's passions is healthy, clean, primal living. Her convictions include organic food, holistic healing, and nurturing relationships with people or animals with positive energy.

Cynthia had been practicing homeopathy for twenty years when she met a woman named Leslie[52] and her horse, Prince Charming.[53] The women developed an instant connection over their love of animals.

---

[52] Name has been changed to protect privacy.
[53] Name has been changed to protect privacy.

Leslie had sold Prince Charming to a man across the country. Before his transport, the Belgian Warmblood received the obligatory vaccination to travel. Shortly thereafter, he collapsed and landed in animal ICU en route to his new home. After treatment, he was able to complete the journey, but even after his arrival, something wasn't quite right.

His new owner treated Prince well, but his ultimate goal was to win blue ribbons, so when Prince damaged his hock, the man planned to euthanize him. Leslie pleaded with him to return the horse to her instead. Upon the gelding's return to Florida, he resumed winning ribbons, until his next vaccination, when he collapsed again.

Leslie still hoped to find a suitable adoptive family for Prince Charming. The right owner needed to have the financial means to properly care for his medical conditions. Cynthia was a perfect match and Leslie turned him over to her. Having little horse experience, but equipped with her incredible passion for animals, Cynthia dove headfirst into a relationship with her new guy.

She explored the various horse-training techniques and settled on the natural Parelli method, choosing Marc as her trainer. The novice began gaining confidence and soon she was well on her way to establishing her bond with Prince.

As time ticked away, one remaining detail continued to evade Cynthia. Leslie had shrugged off the actual legal transfer of the horse, leading to tremendous strain between the women. Cynthia had taken over Prince Charming both financially and emotionally, but Leslie never signed the bill of sale.

After weeks of their deteriorating relationship, Leslie finally admitted that the previous man still technically owned Prince Charming, therefore, she wasn't legally able to offer him to Cynthia. Showing no remorse, Leslie took the offense. "He gave me the horse. I'm not asking him for his signature or the papers. You're just going to have to trust me," she said stone-faced. Cynthia had been hoodwinked.

Shortly thereafter, any remaining shreds of a friendship disintegrated and Cynthia returned the responsibility of her beloved Prince Charming's care to Leslie. She was heartbroken and devastated to lose him. She'd invested over a year of her life and a bucket of money chasing a shadow. She had taken a class to learn the Masterson Method, an integrative technique to help a horse relieve tension, to soothe Prince Charming's old injuries. She had already signed up for the five-day advanced class when everything crumbled.

She commiserated with her trainer, Marc. "We'll find you a horse," he assured her. "Let's start with a rescue. I'll call Shawn." Cynthia didn't know who we were exactly, although a friend had once said, "When you're done with your five-day Masterson class, you should go to RVR and work on their horses." At the time, we were just three initials to her.

When Marc called me, he explained that he had a student in need of a horse and then described Cynthia's holistic approach. It didn't take me more than a few seconds to match Cynthia's background to a deserving animal: Mona Lisa. Her recovery was essentially complete, and she recently received a glowing review from Sergio. She had tolerated treatment of her terrible proud flesh wounds beautifully. I felt Mona Lisa would be a good candidate for holistic medicine and that it could benefit her greatly.

Within a few minutes, Marc called Cynthia back. "She's got the perfect horse for you," he told her. "It's Mona Lisa." Cynthia melted. Her talented son was studying art in Florence, Italy. How fitting was it for her to have a horse named Mona Lisa?

Cynthia and Marc came to RVR the following day. The sky opened up, releasing its contents on the pair, but even the downpour couldn't dampen Cynthia's enthusiasm. They introduced themselves to Mona Lisa at her stall and then Marc turned her out into the paddock. After a moment of hesitation, she approached Cynthia, who immediately saw a long-term future with the dark bay mare.

Within a couple of days, Cynthia finalized the "Sponsor to Adopt" paperwork. Shortly thereafter, Mona Lisa was released for adoption and became Cynthia's first official horse. As always, she charged full steam ahead with her new girl and came to RVR daily to establish a bond.

Of course, Cynthia was informed of the circumstances of Mona Lisa's rescue and she was as impressed as anyone who heard the story. Knowing that Mona Lisa's rescuer, Juan, had not been able to visit the mare he'd risked his life to save, Cynthia offered to reunite the pair by transporting the young hero back and forth herself. Juan jumped on the offer and Cynthia was honored and thrilled to witness their tender reunion at the ranch.

Meanwhile, Mona Lisa befriended another OTTB named Flattering Irene, who began tagging along while Cynthia hung out with her Mona. Irene's similarity to Prince Charming instantly endeared her to Cynthia, and her plan to eventually get Mona Lisa a buddy was expedited. Flattering Irene became Mona Lisa's forever sister when Irene's adoption was finalized a week later. The adoption decision hadn't been taken lightly, as Irene's injuries have resulted in severe osteoarthritis that Cynthia will attempt to treat homeopathically. Her goal is to prove the vet's prediction wrong that Irene will be lame in two years.

Cynthia's girls are undergoing several alternative modalities to promote healing, such as joint supplement CMO (cetyl myristoleate), cold laser (light wavelengths) and microcurrent (low-level electrical currents).

Cynthia has faith that both Mona Lisa and Irene can be fully healed. Faith and a heart the size of Texas. And twelve dogs, three cats, two parrots, and now two horses. But who's counting?

Equine therapy has been successfully integrated into treatment programs for adults and teens who are being treated for substance abuse, addiction, behavior disorders, mood disorders, eating disorders, learning differences, ADD/ADHD, autism, Asperger's, grief/loss, trauma, sex addiction, compulsive gambling, bipolar, depression, and related conditions. [54]

CHAPTER 38

It's a beautiful experience to witness the recovery of a lost cause like Mona Lisa, and even more gratifying to see a loving human like Cynthia fall in love and adopt a restored animal. Feel-good endings help counterbalance the pain and suffering we often see. That's why many of our people were drawn to Taylor Breen's unconventional mission. His attempt to orchestrate a connection between a girl and a horse separated by more than half a continent was a magnet for our caring people.

PeanutButterCup had been a therapy horse for a child with cerebral palsy before falling into abusive hands and finally finding his way into Marianne's care. Marianne was using him as a lesson horse, but his personality was more suited to a one-on-one relationship. The revolving door of unfamiliar riders typical for a lesson horse or trail horse just wasn't his thing.

He was a perfect match for someone just like Sam, and Sam seemed to be the perfect match for him. When Marianne saw Taylor's Facebook posts on "Sam Loves Horses," she contacted him immediately.

---

[54] CRC Heath Group. "What is Equine Therapy?" www.crchealth.com/types-of-therapy/what-is-equine-therapy/ (accessed 8/23/15).

Walinda was tickled pink by the offer of PeanutButterCup. Sam had ridden therapy horses as part of her treatment. The muscles used in horseback riding are often those that need to be strengthened in cerebral palsy patients. Their plan was taking shape.

Back at RVR, Debbie M. made a contribution to the fund and shared the information to encourage others to help as well. She learned from the fund-raiser description that PeanutButterCup was living at a ranch in Florida, so she inquired about his exact location. Of all the places in Florida that he might have been, he was in . . . Riverview. Amazingly, only a few miles away from us.

Meanwhile, Sam's family arranged a trip to meet PeanutButterCup at Marianne's ranch. It was critical they determine if Sam and PeanutButterCup were compatible before the deal was closed, to ensure there wouldn't be any unforeseen issues. Sam was told she was going to meet a horse, and she was, but the true intention of the trip remained a secret. It would be a surprise she'd never forget.

This fairytale was falling into place, but there was a time constraint threatening to foil the plan. Marianne was moving and needed to vacate her premises by August 15. The clock was ticking.

Taylor's wish for Sam and PeanutButterCup's story to go viral was granted. Within days, newspapers and TV stations were publicizing the Facebook page and the fund-raising effort. Donations to the cause flooded the site. Within only a few hours, a single donor from RVR pledged $2,000, the entire estimated amount of the transportation costs. Fund-raisers to support the fund-raiser sprouted up as people joined the bandwagon for this touching and unique cause.

Based on Taylor's original request, drawings from around the globe filled his email inbox. Most were of horses, but some artists also included a drawing of Sam. The receipt of each act of kindness was recognized in the "Sam Loves Horses" Facebook posts. The little girl from Wyoming had become an overnight sensation.

Debbie M. and Sam remained unofficial pen pals. Debbie M.'s newly established role as Sam's horse mentor would prove helpful as Sam would soon have PeanutButterCup, although she didn't know it.

The RVR family joined the movement and several of their children contacted Sam on their own. Debbie M. remained the liaison to the family by maintaining regular contact with Taylor in addition to her exchanges with Sam.

Within days of Marianne's offer of PeanutButterCup, Sam's family arrived in Clearwater Beach, Florida, where Sam was looking forward to seeing the ocean for the first time. It had been less than one month since Walinda's request for a simple horse drawing, and now the family had traveled across the country to introduce Sam to a horse that would potentially become hers.

Debbie M. extended an invitation for Sam and her family to visit our ranch after they met PeanutButterCup at Marianne's. They reached an agreement that the family would attend a celebration with their RVR fans after the meeting.

Debbie M. and fellow volunteer Tammy scrambled to secure a dinner venue with only two days' notice. They settled on J & J Pizza for the event and local company Morningstar Electric subsidized the cost of the food. Everyone seemed to be stepping up to help.

When Debbie M. learned of the family's arrival at Clearwater Beach, she informed them that Winter, the bottlenose dolphin from the movie *Dolphin Tale*, was the star attraction at the nearby Clearwater Marine Aquarium. The facility isn't just any run-of-the-mill aquarium. Its unique mission of Rescue,

Rehab, and Release was the reason that Winter ended up there in the first place. She's famously known for the prosthetic tail she wears after her original one was damaged beyond repair in a crab trap.

Thrilled with Debbie M.'s suggestion, Sam, her brother, and their parents visited Winter the following morning. What Debbie M. hadn't realized when she suggested the aquarium is that Sam had struggled considerably with the braces she needed for her uncooperative legs. She'd fallen in love with the dolphin after seeing Winter's heart-wrenching but successful adjustment to her prosthetic tail, a highlight of the movie. She'd recognized Winter's struggle as being similar to her own. These kindred spirits were both determined to fight through their adversity and Sam was elated to meet Winter in person. Debbie M. had hit a home run without even realizing it!

Unfortunately, Sam was feeling sick by that afternoon, so they returned to the hotel to rest. Bad turned to worse when she later developed a fever. The family took a trip to the local emergency room, where she was admitted overnight for observation. Sadly, health crises were not unusual for the family.

The following morning, Sam was discharged from the hospital, allowing the family to rest for the day before the scheduled meeting with PeanutButterCup at Marianne's ranch that afternoon.

Thankfully, by the appointed time, Sam was well enough to make the hour-long trip to meet a new friend. Taylor had arranged for a Tampa News affiliate to be there to film the much-anticipated meeting.

Sam was adorable, as always. Her beautiful, long blond curls were swept across her forehead and fastened with a bushy white bow. A large blue horse face adorned her white tee shirt, a perfect choice for the event. Her walker, decked out in hot pink-and-black zebra stripes, was befitting of a rock star.[55]

When the big moment finally arrived and she met PeanutButterCup, Sam was smitten. "I thought it was adorable," she told the on-hand reporter.

After their introduction, Marianne offered Sam a ride, and of course she was delighted to oblige. When his new friend was placed securely on his back, PeanutButterCup demonstrated the calm and gentle disposition of a perfect therapy animal. He followed the lead gracefully for a few turns around the pasture, carrying his precious cargo with care. He stopped on a dime, obeying flawlessly.

Marianne flashed Sam a full grin. The ride had gone off without a hitch. Sam's crooked crash helmet dwarfed her pretty face as she looked down at Marianne from her perch atop PeanutButterCup. It was a picture-perfect moment and a glorious achievement.

"Let me ask you something," Marianne said to Sam. "Would you like to take PeanutButterCup home?"

Sam stared, frozen in stunned silence, while she tried to comprehend this unbelievable change of events.

"Did you just get a pony?" her mom asked her. And as the realization took hold, Sam's smile lit up the scene. "I think you did!" Walinda confirmed.

"Samantha, what do you think about the horse?" she continued.

"I love it," Sam said, drawing laughter and cheers from the small crowd.

"They got along perfectly from the moment that they met. You could tell there was an instant bond of understanding between the two," Taylor told the newspaper reporter. "It's all a

---

[55] Taken from Tampa News Affiliate video

breath of fresh air to see so many people who don't even know each other come together with only one goal: to make one very special little girl smile."

The day had been a smashing success but one more item remained on the agenda. The RVR supporters awaited the family's arrival with bated breath at the appointed restaurant. It was well after 6 p.m. when Taylor arrived and broke the news that Sam's brother had fallen ill so the family had adjourned to Clearwater for the evening.

Disappointed but not defeated, the group continued their festivities, even in the absence of the guest of honor.

Although they were nearly neighbors and both heavily involved with horses, Marianne had not interacted with RVR before. The gathering gave Debbie M. the opportunity to meet Marianne, the woman who had triggered this remarkable event, in person.

The evening hadn't turned out as planned, but the mood remained upbeat. People celebrated the beauty of Sam and PeanutButterCup's story, which they had helped to realize.

. . .

Now that the meeting of Sam and PeanutButterCup had proven successful and it was certain that Sam's family would be taking the horse, the issue of Marianne needing to vacate her property became an urgent priority.

Taylor was concerned about running out of time at Marianne's before PeanutButterCup's transportation could be finalized, so he secured temporary boarding. PeanutButterCup was moved thirty miles away to a facility belonging to a friend of Taylor's. He would remain safely there while he waited for his ride to Wyoming.

*Horses are naturally neophobic, that is,
afraid of new things, and since the average
horse trailer has a dark interior, poor or
insecure footing, and an unstable ramp
system, many horses can become paralyzed
with fear. Horses acquire trailering problems
primarily through improper training or bad
experiences.*[56]

CHAPTER 39

Between Taylor's initiative and Marianne's horse, we were witnessing a heartwarming story unfolding before us. However, Marianne was facing a strict deadline to vacate her property, and that affected several horses besides PeanutButterCup. By her final day, everyone had been moved except Gigi, and Marianne was panic-stricken. She'd been trying unsuccessfully for two days to get the obstinate mare loaded on a trailer. In her desperation, she placed an SOS call to her new friends at RVR to see if we would help.

"Come load her. I can't take it anymore," Marianne pleaded. Because of her agitated state and how she described the frazzled condition of the horse, I thought we might need some backup. LeRoy offered to help, so he, Debbie S., and I took off.

It was a typical steamy summer Florida day, and Marianne was melting. Her crimson cheeks, glossy face, and moistened clothing proved Gigi had gotten the best of her. "I can't do anything with her," she kept repeating.

---

[56] Western College of Veterinary Medicine at the University of Saskatchewan. "Trailering Problems in Horses. www.usask.ca/wcvm/herdmed/applied-ethology/behaviourproblems/trailer.html (accessed 8/23/15).

Gigi was lathered and pacing. Agitated. Terrified. Whatever trauma had been unraveling there for the prior two days had brought both horse and owner to their knees.

First, we pushed back the paddock gate, then pulled the trailer up to span the opening, giving Gigi no option but to load. She wanted absolutely nothing to do with that trailer. We then moved the trailer away and walked Gigi around the area, pacing her on laps past the vehicle. Usually after a horse has passed by the trailer once, they will load on the following lap. Not Gigi. Next we applied a butt strap to corral her near the trailer. We coaxed her with food and she took the bait until she placed one front hoof on the trailer, then immediately reared straight up, slamming her head into the roof.

That was the final straw. I couldn't get Gigi loaded and I conceded. Normally loading any horse is a snap for me, but I'd met my match with this challenger. Fear glazed her wild rolled eyes. She'd risked flipping backward or damaging her sensitive poll, much like hitting a person on the top of their head has potential for serious harm. She was clearly willing to do everything in her power to stay off that trailer. When it came down to her potentially injuring herself or someone else, I knew we couldn't take any more chances. Besides, I'd pulled every rabbit out of my hat in the hour and a half we'd been trying.

The rattled Marianne was beside herself. "I need to leave. I can't take this anymore," she repeated. Once she realized it was unlikely we'd be able to load Gigi, she summoned her vet to put the frantic mare down. It was her last resort and he was on the way.

I had to leave for an appointment, so I told Debbie S. to keep the truck and trailer and do whatever they needed to do. Debbie S. started packing up, but LeRoy stood resolved. "I'm not leaving her. I know what her fate is if I do," he said and proceeded to try again and again to get her to load.

Seeing that LeRoy was getting nowhere and the vet would be arriving at any moment, Debbie S. thought of one last ditch idea.

"The next option is to walk her," she told LeRoy.

"I'm walking her then," he said.

They consulted Marianne to gauge how Gigi might handle the road traffic.

"She's crazy," Marianne said, but this didn't deter LeRoy.

"I'm saving this horse today," he told Debbie S. There was no negotiating with him.

Debbie S. alerted me to LeRoy's plan and as I took the sharp curve on Rhodine Drive, a terrible feeling told me that something bad was going to happen to them. I called Debbie S. back to warn her.

Premonition or not, LeRoy's mind was set. "I'm taking her. I don't care if I have to walk *around* Rhodine Drive and it takes all night." I had told LeRoy that although Gigi was not an RVR rescue horse, he could board her there, and that became his destination. The shortest route back to the ranch would be about six miles. If they diverted around Rhodine Drive, it would add hours to their trip.

While Debbie S. got Marianne to sign the paperwork, LeRoy and Gigi slipped away, becoming specks in the distance.

Debbie S. caught up, hauling the empty trailer, and gave LeRoy the game plan. She would drive behind him with the blinkers on, then pass and cut off traffic coming from the opposite direction. She'd keep repeating that until they reached the ranch.

Most of the streets were two-lane secondary roads, with little or no shoulder, where drivers normally zip right along. The muggy Florida heat quickly taxed LeRoy and he stripped off his soaking tee shirt.

"Y'all need any help?" concerned passersby kept asking. Their perplexed glances bobbed back and forth between the empty trailer and the sweaty man and his horse inching along either behind or in front of it.

"Oh no, we're all set! Just walking the horse!" Debbie S. shouted out to them.

As they approached the curve on Rhodine Drive I had warned them about, Debbie S. saw the blind spot just beyond a pasture of bulls. She warned LeRoy as she pulled up ahead in their orchestrated dance. This time she planted the truck sideways, blocking the entire road. She'd stop traffic until Gigi made it safely around the blind spot. Irate semitruck drivers lost patience quickly, blasting their horns and flailing their arms, but Debbie S. sat still, refusing to be intimidated.

One bull that had been lying down got up and began walking toward the road, although he was contained behind a wire fence. Sure enough, when Gigi spotted the approaching predator, she leapt out into the road, pulling LeRoy like a feather. It was the tragedy I had anticipated, only Debbie S. had ensured no traffic would harm them and LeRoy was able to quickly settle his girl.

She followed his lead past the bull, cowering behind LeRoy as much as a horse can tuck behind a thin man. Her fear was palpable, but she followed dutifully. Debbie S. watched in amazement as a rock-solid trust was building with each step.

Three long hours after they'd begun, they arrived to a welcoming committee at the ranch. Gigi's eyes glazed with fear when LeRoy began removing the ropes. Her security net was slipping away.

"Where are you going? What are you doing?" she seemed to plead. Once untethered, she still stuck to his every move.

LeRoy had literally risked his life to save hers and she seemed to understand that. In the coming days, Gigi became

Kahlia, meaning "Lucky One," and I don't think there could have been a more fitting name for this blessed mare.

"You know how I hate to stand in front of the camera . . .
I stood in front of 10 cameras to tell your story. I wanted justice and I didn't care what the ramifications would be. I believe I paid a price for fighting for you and I would do it again and again and again. I vowed to be the voice for the voiceless . . . I will continue. I love you, little guy."

—Shawn Jayroe

CHAPTER 40

Marianne had gotten stuck in a jam with Kahlia, and the mare had been fortunate LeRoy was willing to help. Marianne's situation was one of those unfortunate circumstances in life that aren't necessarily foreseeable or preventable.

Animal cruelty, on the other hand, is a conscious ugly reality. One way that I believe we can curtail the despicable actions is to shine a spotlight on the problem. Greater public awareness has the potential to exert pressure on government agencies to tighten cruelty laws. At times, we see perpetrators of our abused rescues brought to justice, but too many times we don't. In any case, we do our part to fight for these animals who have no voice.

One of our most significant cases began when a local veterinarian was called to euthanize a horse in Plant City that had supposedly fallen off a porch. He immediately became suspicious about the claim when he arrived at the property. Of the four miniature horses there, all were in various stages of starvation and neglect, but two were far worse than the others. The vet refused to put down the horse, but called us instead.

Little Warrior hovered at death's door. The horse that had supposedly "fallen off the porch" had actually been starved to the point of collapse. He simply lay motionless on the ground.

I've been rescuing horses for so long that I think I've seen it all, but sometimes the human capacity for evil still astounds me. Every case of clear neglect and abuse angers me, but I was enraged when I came on this horrific scene. Warrior had been tied on a patch of sand where he'd crumpled. No food, water, or even grass were within his reach. He was tiny. Miniature horses are normally fat little butterballs at 350 to 400 pounds. Warrior weighed half that. His dark drab coat draped over his bones, showing every contour. It was tragic.

Unfortunately, we've seen too many cases of this type of abuse. What made this one even more detestable was this baby was losing his life only steps away from the owner's porch. She literally had a front-row seat to watch him waste away to a slow, cruel death.

Miniature horses don't require much food to keep their compact bodies healthy. A measly cup of food a day, or about $10 a week, is all it takes. Knowing how long Warrior endured the starvation just infuriated me. I can't understand or accept the mentality of someone who can treat a supposed pet that way.

We had to threaten the owner with a criminal investigation before she agreed to surrender all the minis. There was no way we were leaving with any of them still in her care.

It was out of the question for Warrior to walk to the trailer, but four of us were easily able to lift him using a sling. He barely budged with the movement. His head perked up out of curiosity, but he was otherwise a pile of dead weight. Fear and confusion clouded his eyes, although he settled into the back of the truck quickly.

He warmly accepted the love and compassion we showered on him. I guessed that the attention and affection he received in those minutes once he was in our care were the most he'd seen in years.

We carted his buddies Spirit, Sandy, and Sandy's colt, Lily back to RVR for their recovery as well, although none were as desolate as Warrior.

At the ranch, we dove right into Warrior's treatment. His neglected hoofs had overgrown to the point of being ridiculous. They'd grown four inches longer than they should have been, making it nearly impossible for him to stand until the farrier clipped them.

He gobbled up the bits of hay we offered during his exam—probably the first food he'd eaten in a very long time. Our compassionate volunteers rubbed his back, kissed his nose, ran fingers through his black mane, and willed him to live.

His dim eyes were glazed over and he could barely move, but Warrior licked our outstretched hands and nudged them with his nose. He accepted the love we gave and reciprocated in kind. His previous owner had nearly killed him, but Warrior still continued to love.

The pathetic little guy was barely present. His abuse had gone so far beyond tolerable that he mostly just laid still. We worked in shifts, turning Warrior over manually every couple of hours. It took several of us to hoist him up and steady him on his feet. He could stand for only fifteen minutes at a time before he'd collapse from exhaustion.

After two days, we found another horse rescue, Beauty's Haven, near Ocala, who had a sling small enough for Warrior. The sling would allow us to suspend him, but it meant we'd have to commute nearly two hours to maintain his care. But, as I've always seen, people stepped up to the challenge. After we transported Warrior to Beauty's Haven, we spent another two days nursing him in his new upright position.

But it wasn't enough. Fourteen-year-old Warrior lost his remaining shred of life only four days after his rescue. We had given our all despite the towering odds stacked against the poor boy.

The ensuing criminal investigation confirmed that two of the four horses we'd taken had been deprived of food for a year. Thankfully, all three of the other minis went on to make a full recovery and were adopted into loving forever homes.

Warrior's owner was charged with felony and misdemeanor counts of animal cruelty. I was grateful for the action taken, but it hadn't gone far enough. How had such long-term, deliberate, despicable abuse not warranted any jail time? I couldn't tolerate the injustice and the false spin that the owner put on the story when it hit the media.

I vowed to find justice for Warrior—perhaps this was why the veterinarian called to put Warrior down had contacted me instead of his local rescue. Did he know I'd fight for the justice that Warrior deserved?

Unfortunately, the breaking of the story basically turned into a political exposé of sorts. I was little David crushing giant Goliath's toes. But I didn't care. We pushed until Warrior's story went global on social media and every news outlet, garnering support from as far away as New Zealand and Paris.

I understood my role as a horse rescuer wouldn't always be met with support and appreciation, especially with the controversial and confrontational aspects. However, I don't suppose I fully realized the danger it might bring to me, either.

I fight for justice for the horses and to bring change to a society that ignores the abuse. I always begin by using the proper channels, but sometimes the crimes are just too egregious and I do whatever it takes, including using the media, to try to bring about awareness and change.

My techniques proved successful as far as bringing awareness to RVR and our mission and increasing the number of supporters to our cause. The flip side was that greater awareness meant shining a light onto a sometimes dark and inadequate judicial system that allowed people to mistreat these animals without sufficient repercussion.

Maybe it was purely coincidence and maybe it wasn't, but shortly after we pushed out Warrior's tragic story to the media, I found myself slapped with a lawsuit and defending myself in kangaroo court. There were legal charges of neglect brought against RVR that were such a farce it was laughable, only it wasn't funny at all. The reputation we had worked so hard to build was being dragged through the mud with completely false allegations, and I seemed powerless to stop it.

The media loves a train wreck and we became a headline for all the wrong reasons. The smear campaign against me and RVR went global, and I feared we would be destroyed.

*One in three returning troops is diagnosed
with serious posttraumatic stress symptoms.
Less than 40 percent will seek help.*[57]

CHAPTER 41

I had seen adversity in my years, but having our reputation called into question was devastating. The case wasn't thrown out of court even though the claims were so twisted and ludicrous that I had to assume I was being set up out of retaliation. After receiving threats, I added security at the property to ensure my family's safety. I became paranoid at the sight of any newcomers at the ranch. Where they part of a setup? With all the volunteers coming and going, who could I trust? I was skeptical of anyone's intention unless I knew the person well before the media blitz.

But I'm a fighter, and life marched on. There were horses in trouble who needed our help. As our reputation in the community and beyond had grown, so did the requests to take in horses. Scenarios ranged from those who were moving and couldn't take their horses, to those in financial distress who couldn't afford to feed or care for their horses any longer. We stood by our mission to take only those in dire abusive or neglected situations, but also realized we could use our growing network of horse lovers to facilitate rehoming other horses in need.

An individual horse owner looking to rehome their animal didn't have access to many people who might be interested to adopt a horse, but we did. And thus began our Rehome Network, managed through our Facebook page.

---

[57] PTSD Foundation of America. "The Statistics." http://ptsdusa.org/what-is-ptsd/the-statistics/ (accessed 8/23/15).

The description reads as follows: "Due to the fact that RVR Horse Rescue cannot take in all horses, we have designed this courtesy listing as a place to post horses looking for good homes. RVR does not guarantee the health, soundness, or temperament of the horses posted below. These horses have not been evaluated by an RVR Horse Rescue representative. RVR Horse Rescue is not responsible for the details listed with each horse, and it does not have knowledge of the horse owner's credentials. Please contact the owner directly."

Owners needing to rehome a horse will send us the pertinent information and pictures, which we post on our site. Parties interested in a horse can monitor this site and contact the owner—kind of like eBay for horses. The process requires little effort on our part and potentially prevents horses from being discarded and needing to be rescued later.

Sometimes when we get a call about a placement, we have a potential family already in mind and a transaction occurs seamlessly. When I learned about an owner who needed to rehome Sunny and Buddy, I knew exactly who to call.

Nathan and his family began volunteering at RVR with the hope of adopting a horse. Nathan was a United States Marine veteran, having devoted thirteen years of his life to protect our country. Fighting in Operation Iraqi Freedom and Operation Enduring Freedom left invisible but profound scars. Horrific memories haunted him. Well-meaning civilians encouraged him to just "pick up and move on." But Nathan just couldn't erase the grisly memories of his military missions and neither his family nor friends could even begin to comprehend the demons that tortured his thoughts. He was stuck between these two worlds.

After his honorable discharge, Nathan and his family settled in Riverview and became like any typical American family. Nathan, his wife, Amanda, and their three children scurried around between work, school, extracurriculars, and other social activities. They'd converge back at the house late in the day, drop into bed exhausted, then repeat over and over. They were wearing out the hamster wheel while losing touch with each other and missing out on the real beauty of life.

Their friends often sung the praises of horse ownership and how enriching it could be for children or an entire family. Nathan and Amanda considered the possibility of adopting a horse, although Nathan wasn't completely sold on the idea. He had grown up around horses, but had never established a real connection with them.

Their friends referred them to RVR and they arrived in search of a horse for the family. After attending an orientation, they spent many weeks volunteering while trying to establish a relationship with an animal to adopt. Their arrival at the ranch occurred during my heightened skepticism of newcomers and I welcomed them but at an arm's length. How could I know if they were for real?

Once I saw that Nathan was coming on a regular basis and that his family seemed genuinely interested in a horse, I let my guard down and welcomed them in. They needed a good starter horse for their children, whose ages ranged from seven to eleven years old. The horses they preferred either already had sponsors, making them unavailable, or needed a seasoned handler.

I became aware of a man who was relocating and needed to rehome two horses in nearby Plant City. The owner described the horses as being in excellent condition, so I immediately thought of Nathan's family. However when Nathan went to retrieve them he found an altogether different scene.

Buddy and Sunny were in a pathetic state and desperate for food. Sunny had been chewing on the side of a mobile home, and Buddy had been eating dirt and his own poop. Nathan was shocked to see the condition of the boys and he provided us with photos confirming their actual appearance. Our mission changed from a simple rehoming to rehabilitation when we loaded both the geldings on a trailer two days later and delivered them to RVR. Although our original plan for rehoming hadn't worked out perfectly, we still established a connection between horses that needed a home and an interested family.

After their weigh-in, we found Buddy and Sunny were both approximately 400 pounds underweight. They had significant challenges to overcome. Sunny had developed compulsive cribbing that led to a choking incident, whereas Buddy suffered for weeks with life-threatening colic as his digestive system rebelled against the dirt and poop he had consumed. Thankfully, a U7 supplement recommended by the vet improved Buddy's colic, at which point we could shift the focus to getting the sand out of his system.

Within a month it was clear the horses were conquering their battles. Both were plumping back to size and their bad habits gradually waned. Nathan and his family poured love on the two new guys, but still had a difficult decision to make as to whether they wanted—and could afford—both of them. But watching Sunny and Buddy struggle for their lives endeared them to the family members, who chose to move forward with their original plan of adoption and take them both.

As for Nathan personally, his experiences in war had trapped him in isolation. He hid behind his warrior's shield, never feeling safe enough to drop the guard.

Veteran's Day is typically a day of reflection for him, and it generally invokes a host of mixed emotions. Nathan and Amanda decided a visit with their equine children might be just the medicine Nathan needed.

Upon their arrival, Amanda split off to visit with Sunny while Nathan joined Buddy at the hay feeder. Without warning, Nathan tossed his warrior's shield to the ground, then literally climbed inside the large open wooden box, nestled back into the prickly cushion, and vented all the emotional junk that had been bearing down on him. Compassion poured from Buddy's gazing eyes as he gave Nathan his undivided attention between nibbles of hay.

In those tender moments, Nathan's tough shell began to soften and he knew he had a true friend. Nathan now understood completely the connection he heard about but had never attained with his childhood horse. Buddy reached the guarded Marine in a way no one else had.

When Buddy tired of eating and listening, he began blowing hay at Nathan, creating a playful game that immediately brought a smile to the grateful soldier. The breakthrough between a man and his horse that day was only the beginning of their beautiful relationship. Nathan continues to chat with Buddy whenever he needs someone to listen, and Buddy is always right there waiting.

> *RVR Horse Rescue Inc received the Top-Rated NonProfit award from GreatNonProfits in 2015.*[58]

CHAPTER 42

It's a heavenly experience to witness life-changing breakthroughs between the horses and their humans. The more I taste the sweet successes, the hungrier I become to accomplish more. As a business owner, I always strive to keep moving forward and improving. As I continued to refine and grow the operations at the ranch, I employed the same philosophy that helped to make my salon a success.

The difference at the ranch is that every cent is donated, requiring the generosity of the community to keep us afloat. Monthly expenses are monumental at over $12,000 between food, medical, and farrier costs. And not one cent goes to the all-volunteer staff, myself included. Each time I worry that I won't be able to pay the bills, let alone to keep making improvements, God keeps providing.

A man approached me one day and said, "I read a story about you and I'm really interested in helping you out. Here's five hundred dollars." When I have faith that it will come, it always does. Other grants and specific fund-raisers have kept us afloat and allowed me to keep inching forward.

There are several ways for people to help us help the horses and I think we've summarized the options well: If you can't adopt, FOSTER. If you can't foster, SPONSOR. If you can't sponsor, VOLUNTEER. If you can't volunteer, DONATE. If you can't donate, NETWORK.

---

[58]Great Nonprofits. "RVR Horse Rescue." http://greatnonprofits.org/org/rvr-horse-rescue (accessed 8/23/15).

It's my favorite plea, because it shows that even without time or money, people can help us by sharing our information with a click of a button. Each click helps us reach people who might be interested to help. Our donors and supporters are the muscular legs and feet beneath us that keep propelling us forward.

In the spirit of continual improvement of the ranch operations, I decided to build a barn out back. It would be run independently of the rescue, but enable me to help more horses. Thirty stalls would provide some steady income from boarding, allowing me to reduce my hours at the salon so I could devote more time to the ranch.

I pictured the barn sitting beyond the pond and pasture at the back of the property. From my back porch, I would be able to observe the herd, albeit through the brush and trees that encircled the pond. I dreamt of pastures full of second-chance horses, and that vision became cemented in my mind.

Not one to sit around and wait, I grabbed the tractor and started leveling the land where the barn would be built. Word of my plan spread to the volunteers and my far-fetched idea drew considerable ribbing.

"She's got some testosterone," one joked.

They all chuckled at my expense. The crazy lady was at it again.

But, as usual, I was dead serious and determined. The intense willpower I inherited from my father had gotten me this far in life. I didn't have one penny to get me started, but that wouldn't stop me. I had already visualized the end result.

And as I cleared the land, I spoke to God as I always do. Well, at first I did more than speak. I pleaded and begged to the point of desperation for weeks. I needed His help to achieve my newly devised plan and to remove some of the burden I felt constantly bearing down on me. Now that I had a new mission, the wheels spun in overdrive. Constant planning, worrying, and rationalizing consumed me.

After several weeks of fretting, I finally made a conscious decision to stop my chaotic spiral and grasp my faith instead. As we are instructed in Psalm 37:7, "Be still before the Lord and wait patiently for Him." I took this message to heart and turned my attitude around completely. *Be still*, I told myself. Instead of the panicking madwoman that I had been, I sat still and was patient—a complete departure from my norm.

Shortly thereafter I granted an interview that would be published in a women's magazine. Grateful for any publicity that helps spread our message, I was happy to oblige. After the interview, we began a conversation off the record.

"So what's your ultimate goal?" Carole asked me, referring to the ranch and rescue.

I divulged my dream to build the thirty-stall barn and explained how it would help me enhance the rescue operation.

She thought for a moment before asking, "Well, why don't we make that happen? Would fifty thousand dollars be enough to get you started?"

She nearly bowled me over. An angel disguised as a reporter had just waltzed into my life. Her offer surpassed anything I could have imagined. My prayers and pleas on the tractor had been answered. I had been still and patient, and God was providing.

The beautiful new barn allowed me to begin a boarding facility, reserved only for horses rescued and rehabilitated through RVR. Handled as a separate business, Heart to Heart allows me to offer low boarding fees for the adopted rescues, an attractive incentive for potential adopters and for inexperienced horse owners. The boarding facility pays monthly rent to RVR, keeping the rescue afloat.

The trade-off from my original vision was that the addition of the barn didn't allow me to cut my hours at the salon significantly. With the reduced boarding rates, Heart to Heart barely stands on its own financially. But when I see the stalls full of adopted rescues and the camaraderie of the adoptive parents and their babies, I know the trade-off was a good one.

Other changes we make at the ranch generally originate from needs we discover as we treat the rescues, as was the case with Sara.

Dr. Gold requested that we help an injured racehorse he was certain would be euthanized. His heart had gone out to the beautiful and sweet Sara. "I will help you with her medical care, but you need to take her," he requested.

Sara's X-rays showed a small piece of protruding bone that Dr. Gold surmised could be surgically pushed back into place and fastened with a screw. Although her racing career was certainly over, surgery would fix the problem.

She couldn't stand with the injury and we had no way to keep her upright. She needed to be supported by a sling, which we didn't have, so we put the word out to the grapevine.

Because I have to squeeze every donated penny, we are not in a position to pay for costly surgery for one animal. Doing so would prevent me from helping many others. However, Brandon Equine stepped up to perform the surgery.

Sara's pre-op X-rays showed more clearly the true extent of her injury. What we thought was a single piece of bone protruding was actually a shattered bone. There would be nothing to screw together. We had no more options for the poor girl, who languished in pain, and we had to put her to rest.

In the meantime, we hustled to plan a fund-raiser for a proper slinging system. The fund-raiser was in honor of Kiwi, another rescue who was too weak to stand on his own. Our manual method required ten people to raise and lower him throughout the day and night.

The fund-raiser allowed us to complete the project, which included a shed with an overhead crane that traverses in and out and pulleys that travel up and down. The color-coded straps of the sling adjust for size and can hold any patient securely. A 1,000-pound animal could be raised or lowered with the push of a button, and the enclosure would keep the patient out of the elements.

My office fills the back of the building and doubles as the medical supply room. There we house various medicines, medical supplies, and meticulous records of any procedure performed on a past or present horse, a number that tallies to more than 200 and counting. Records are sorted by category: Current, Adopted on Property, Adopted off Property, and Deceased.

The completed project was christened as "Sara's House." At the entrance, I used my finger to write a permanent prayer into the drying cement floor: "DEAR LORD, Please Bless Every Horse That Walks Through These Doors. In Jesus's Name. AMEN. Shawn." Alongside, the words "RIP SARA" are enclosed in a heart, putting the final touches on a tribute to a beautiful soul we did our best to save.

The barn and the shed are two examples of projects that expanded our services at the ranch, but I'm also constantly trying to find ways to extend our reach outside the ranch to help more horses in need.

We continue to gain momentum on our C.L.E.A.R initiative and find ways to spread our message. We launched "Charity's Vision" as the official program name, a fitting tribute to our battered first rescue.

Our food and hay bank, Horse Angels, assists people who are struggling to feed their horses. If we can help keep a horse in its home and prevent another emaciated animal from needing to be rescued, I consider it a success.

Our fingers continue to grab opportunities to network within the community. We've opened our doors to foster children and young women saved from human trafficking. These traumatized folks can use the healing power of the rescues at the same time that they provide a necessary pair of hands to our operation.

Our ongoing relationship with the local Girl Scout troop led to the building of our Rainbow Bridge memorial—a wooden arc they created and dedicated to our rescue babies who have crossed over the bridge. An equine shoe in honor of each deceased horse is tacked to the monument after the passing. The bridge flanks Sara's House and is a constant reminder of our lost souls.

We continue to use all social media outlets to extend our reach and impact. Additional websites, such as Petfinder, help extend our audience of potential adoptive families. Our Rehome Network provides a safer alternative to other online sites.

We are reaching out in many different avenues and each one we tackle brings us one step closer to our goal.

More than 100 equine rescue groups held events in 33 states in conjunction with the ASPCA 2015 "Help a Horse Day." The event raised awareness of the work equine rescues and sanctuaries do to save and care for at-risk horses.[59]

CHAPTER 43

Taylor Breen was getting closer to reaching his goal with the help of our volunteers and a legion of supporters across the country. Once he finalized PeanutButterCup's transportation, he breathed a sigh of relief. However, he then became increasingly skeptical about the arrangement. The driver became evasive, noncommittal, and unresponsive. Although the man had agreed to deliver PeanutButterCup to his new home, Taylor was unable to get firm answers and finally had to cancel the deal.

He couldn't take any chances on this shipment. No way. Too many people had a stake in making a little girl's dream come true. He needed another plan.

Angels seemed to be appearing at each turn in this saga. Another one stepped forward in the form of a truck driver. When the man caught wind of the Sam and PeanutButterCup craze, he decided he wanted to help. The story had touched a soft spot in his heart, stemming from a childhood memory of his family's horse ranch. Not only did he want to transport the horse, he donated his services to do it. His generosity would allow the funds that had been raised for the transportation to be applied to the boarding costs in Wyoming instead.

---

[59] ASPCA. "Help a Horse Day 2015." www.aspca.org/get-involved/horses/help-a-horse-day-2015 (accessed 8/23/15).

Shortly thereafter, and as promised, PeanutButterCup arrived safely in Wyoming. The princess made her way outside to welcome her prince to his new home, while their thousands of cyber fans looked on and cheered.

To Sam, PeanutButterCup had simply been a marvelous gift. But to those who witnessed each piece of the elaborate puzzle glide gracefully together, it was nothing short of a miracle. As Taylor had predicted, the uniting of Sam and PeanutButterCup certainly did restore faith in humanity by proving that countless Good Samaritans would reach out to help a complete stranger.

Taylor hopes his example will inspire others to put forth just a little effort to brighten someone else's day. "Everyone can make a difference in this world," Taylor says. "Even if it's just a small one."

But Sam and PeanutButterCup's journey is just another example of the everyday miracles we experience at RVR. In our world, we encounter the dregs of humanity, but also the absolute best of mankind. We witness the goodness of people outweighing the atrocities of others. We experience life, sometimes only a few shallow breaths from death, flourish again through love and compassion. Broken-hearted humans are made whole by loving a broken horse. Cassidy and her amazing Gracie are a beautiful example of such a union.

I invited Cassidy to address our crowd during a Help a Horse Day fund-raiser, a joint effort with the ASPCA. Her Gracie, not a fan of a noisy boisterous crowd, paced in the round pen for her public debut, but quickly settled as Cassidy explained their journey:

> When I began as a volunteer at RVR, my spirit was nearly as shattered as Gracie's withers had been when she first arrived. I didn't know her yet,

of course. It would be a few weeks until I would get to know this very special horse and her story. Until then, I was here to try and keep my hands and my mind busy as I pieced my life back together.

I had fled my home state of Connecticut, the only place I had ever known, just three months prior, the desperate action of someone who had just survived and escaped an almost decade-long abusive relationship. With nothing but a suitcase, my car, and a Google search to guide me, I wound up in Tampa, Florida, newly free, entirely lost, alone, exhilarated, and yet, understandably, terrified. So I did what any good Connecticut farm girl does in a situation like that: I set out to find the horses.

Another Google search led me to RVR, a rescue I knew nothing about and yet felt entirely drawn toward. For a few hours a week, I got to lose myself in the velvet muzzles and mild nickerings of these gentle creatures. I hauled water, mucked poo, and gradually got to know all the incredible people and animals here. It wasn't long, of course, until I longed for a bond with a horse again—it had been almost ten years since my parents had sold the farm I grew up on, and I missed the magic that I had only ever experienced with horses. Beyond that, I was lonely, newly forced to contend with my past in the broad expanses of day and in the wee hours of the night. I needed someone to love.

So I did some hunting around and asked if there was a horse I could sponsor. I was given a list of horses and, being relatively new, didn't really know any of them that well. So I did what any desperate, ignorant horse lover does: I stood at the edge of the paddock, gazed out at each horse, and with hardly a reason, I picked, and I chose Gracie.

I didn't know much about this little sorrel mare, just that she was sensitive about being touched and known amongst the volunteers for nipping. But when I look back at that day, I'm not even sure if that factored into my decision to sponsor her. I knew she was a tough cookie, but it was something about the way she was standing apart from the others, something in her eyes that drew me to her. Looking back, I think I just knew intuitively that she and I were the same in a lot of ways.

What I would learn in the coming months is that Gracie had been brutally ripped apart by another horse kept in too close quarters with her, that she had been neglected, starved, deprived of love, attention, and even basic needs like food and veterinary care. For close to two years she endured the brutalities forced upon her by people who didn't care any more for her than they did a rock, or a grain of sand. What they didn't know is that, unlike a rock, she suffered. Unlike a grain of sand, she felt every flinch of fear and tremor of pain. But, like a rock, she was underestimated, and much, much harder to break.

The incredible people at RVR that saved her learned of this firsthand. Throughout all their dedication and hard work over a span of months, they tended to her gruesome wounds 'round-the-clock, removing pus, fragmented bone, and dead tissue from her broken withers. They stood beside her when the pain of her exposed nerves became too great. And throughout multiple surgeries, even when they feared she might not make it, this miracle horse pulled through. Too emaciated to be put under anesthesia, she stood patiently as veterinarians helped remove the raging infection and piece her back together. It was, as they say, as if she knew they were saving her life.

So it is to those people that I owe the chance I have to be a part of Gracie's new life. Shawn, Lisa, Kit, and so many others who were integral to the process believed this horse could live, and so she did. But it's also due to her own incredible strength and will to survive.

I think that's what I saw that day in the paddock that drew me in: something of a kindred spirit in this beautiful horse that lived through such brutality, endured through so much pain, and came out standing on the other side.

Gracie and I, we are both survivors, and when I envision us, I see us walking side by side through this journey—two gals, a horse and a human, learning to love again in a new place full of heart and healing, a beautiful place known as RVR.

I adopted Gracie on Valentine's Day, 2015—the date an homage to the fact that she is my very reason, my purpose, to becoming whole again, my love and my light as I struggle through the darkness of a past that still threatens to consume me.

RVR saved Gracie, and in turn, this beautiful mare has saved me. We are now a family built by fate, strung together by a love that doesn't just keep us alive, but helps us to thrive as we look forward to whole, new futures.

This is the miracle that happens every time to those who really love: the more they give, the more they possess.
—Rainer Maria Rilke

CHAPTER 44

Cassidy's eloquent speech validates my life's work and motivates me to keep fighting. I'm so passionate about animal rescue that sometimes my beliefs or intentions are misunderstood, but there's one thing that's never misconstrued: my love and compassion for animals, and most specifically, our rescue horses. Anyone who knows me knows my entire life is dedicated to my mission to rescue, rehabilitate, and rehome horses.

That's why the allegations that RVR neglects our rescues were especially preposterous and inciting. My legion of volunteers was as shell-shocked as I was, but they never doubted the integrity of the work we did and they backed me 100 percent. The negative publicity dampened our spirit, but we clung to hope. We all understood the value that we provided to the horses and nothing anyone said or thought would change that.

But we're caring and compassionate human beings, so having our reputation called into question was a painful and damaging experience for everyone involved. The bonds that hold us together began to unravel. Tension permeated the ranch and the normally jovial atmosphere evaporated.

A menacing cloud hovered low overhead, but we carried on with business as usual and our next request for help came in the form of a letter. A little filly was starving to death. Baby Bree's mother had died and Bree had weakened to the point that she couldn't stand for long. The board approved her rescue, but rather than retrieve the horse as we normally do, the Good Samaritans wanted to drop her off at RVR.

I immediately regretted our consent when we opened the trailer and saw the scrawny baby had been left unsecured for her transport, allowing her to slide and bounce around like a pinball. She was beautiful, even as a frail stick figure. White markings spattered her dark face and a dingy brown canvas covered the rest of her bones. Her spindly legs ended at white socks, and her stormy eyes rolled in fear as we helped her exit the trailer. She was so tiny it took only two volunteers to steady and guide her out, while the third stroked her head to show we meant no harm.

The vet came to examine Bree and it was obvious she was very sickly. Her poop was loaded with worms. Normally we wait to de-worm rescues because their emaciated systems can't handle the medicine when they first arrive. But because of Bree's extreme infestation, Dr. Gold advised us to give her a tiny dose.

We fitted her with a bright pink halter, suitable for our new baby girl. As weak as she was, Bree's whinny was insistent, indicating her strong will to fight for her life.

We escorted her into her new stall and posted a sign-up sheet for around-the-clock babysitters. Our amazing angels fought to get a spot. They helped Bree to her feet when she wanted to stand, gave her water, and fed her alfalfa and tiny meals that her fragile system could handle. Most important, she was never alone.

In the following days, stuffed animals accumulated in the stall. They provided soft pillows for the ailing baby and her caregivers, who comforted Bree by lying next to her and embracing her in love.

As one day slipped into the next, I thought we were making progress, that is, until the morning Sandy came in with a long face. Bree had just passed away, she told me. She'd lost her battle after only one week with us.

We were devastated. I requested a necropsy because I needed to know what happened. Had I done something wrong? Could I have saved her? With our spirits so low from the legal suit, this loss seemed even more cruel than usual.

After his testing, the vet confirmed Bree would have died regardless. She'd been too far gone with holes in her lungs and a host of other issues. It was little consolation, but at least I wouldn't always have to wonder.

Many times after we make a rescue, the "rest of the story" comes out, but it's often difficult to really discern the truth in most situations. In Bree's case, we later heard the owner had taken the mom away from her baby, so they could barrel race the dam. The mother hadn't died as we'd originally been told. In any case, there was no proof, which meant nothing legally could be done about it.

Bree was never alone for the week she was in our care. As the reality of her death hit, we realized that our united rally around the ailing filly had melded us back into one invincible force. Our bonds became stronger than ever, and joy returned to the ranch. We credit baby Bree as the angel sent to reunite us.

Our little girl was buried in a place of honor at the front gate of the property. A memorial marks her spot at the road, where symbolic pink horse shoes spell out her name and a cherub statue stands guard over our beloved angel.

With our spirits refueled, we battled against the slanderous allegations of neglect by rallying our growing fan base. My heart melted at the overwhelming response. Support from across the country flooded social media networks, and even those who only knew us through Facebook continued to sing our praises. It seemed as though the smear campaign that I feared would destroy us was actually drawing more people to our cause!

Sometimes God has a really roundabout way of answering prayers, but He seemed to be showing me that nothing could destroy us. We had been tested by the devil, and good had truly triumphed over evil.

The passion that drives me is both a blessing and a curse, but the benefits far outweigh the challenges. God has called me to be the beating heart of this incredible healing haven, and, as our soul, He continues to nourish me.

My wealthy childhood and the heyday of my salon business are distant memories now. My world has evolved to an entirely new planet. Friends and acquaintances from my old life ask me, "What happened to you?"

I still enjoy the finer things in life. I had them once. But if you look at me now, you would never know it. I'm the poorest I've ever been. And yet the richest.

What happened to me? A miracle.

ACKNOWLEDGEMENTS — SHAWN JAYROE

Back when horse rescue was only a dream, I could never have imagined anything as spectacular as RVR Horse Rescue has become. It is only with the support of hundreds, if not thousands, of people, that my dream became a reality. It is impossible to thank everyone for their contribution, and if you are not among those listed below, please forgive my oversight. I am grateful for each person who helps in any way.

I have to begin with thanks to God. He has led me to this point and will continue to guide me to help as many horses as possible and to stem the tide of abuse and neglect of beautiful and magnificent equines.

Forever thanks to my Mom and daughters. Your love and support mean the world to me and give me the strength to keep fighting.

I'm indebted to my father for his drive and determination gene that has helped me persevere through many trials that might have otherwise convinced me to give up.

Thank you to Shirley Alarie and all my Horse Angels who participated in any way on this project. You have all helped me realize my dream of having my story in print.

There are many special angels who have stayed by my side through thick and thin. My past and present RVR board members, lead people, and business specialists make RVR a professional, powerful, and well-oiled business. The fact we have been 100% volunteer to this point continues to astound me. The dedication and grit of the angels that help me run the business are incredible.

Financial support comes in many forms and each one is a godsend and helps us stay afloat. Every penny given or item donated allows us the opportunity to keep helping more animals in need. Thank you to every donor! I am grateful for each of you. Special thanks to one particular angel named Heidi Waber who ALWAYS makes sure the horses don't do without!

Where the rubber meets the road, a legion of angels show up each day in relentless sun or torrential rain to feed, water and muck stalls before showering the current residents with love and attention. I am forever grateful for each pair of hands and big heart that keep our operation running.

Thank you to each adoptive family, that free up the stalls to allow us to keep helping more babies in need.

I am eternally grateful to our incredible medical team. Our professionals and para-professionals perform everyday miracles in saving our babies hovering at the brink. Your work is life-changing.

To every RVR supporter, especially those who stood RVR STRONG in my time of need!! Without you, we could not or would not be as awesome as we are today.

ACKNOWLEDGEMENTS – SHIRLEY ALARIE

Shawn Jayroe, you are the real deal. You are an incredible crusader with a remarkable story of love, determination, dedication, and courage. Knowing you has changed my life. Thank you for allowing me to tell your story. I love you.

To all the RVR Angels, I have never been more proud to be part of a team than I am to be part of the "healing haven" we know as RVR. The work you do is amazing and commendable.

My life has been enriched by knowing you and working alongside you. Keep changing the world one horse at a time.

To the Angels who told me their stories. You represent the many caring, warm, and wonderful people of RVR. Special thanks to Alyssa/Amanda, Barbara, Cassidy, Cynthia, David and Bethany, Dawn, Debbie M., Debbie S., Karen, Kelly/Jillian, Kit, Lisa, MJ, Nathan, Sandy, Sergio, Stacy, and Dr. Kuebelbeck and Pam of Brandon Equine.

A big Thank You to the Horse Angels who stepped up to help me with various aspects of this project, including photos and horse descriptions. Special thanks to Stacy for going "above and beyond" and to Karen for your creative input.

Thank you to Taylor Breen for your remarkable and inspiring story that dovetails beautifully with the RVR mission. It is not often that we see thousands of strangers rally around a cause like they did for yours. Bravo!

Special thanks to my GF, Cindy. I love being on this writing journey with you and I appreciate all your support, including being my loyal beta reader and a great consultant!

Thank you to my newest beta reader, Patti. I appreciate you stepping up to help me, Lil Sis. Love you!

A million thanks to my incredibly supportive husband, Fran. With you by my side, this dream feels possible. Thank you for being my biggest cheerleader, my sounding board, and a dedicated and outstanding beta reader. I love you always.

STAY IN TOUCH WITH US!

See photos at SHIRLEYALARIE.COM, A HEALING HAVEN tab.

FOLLOW RVR Horse Rescue: Facebook, Twitter, Instagram, www.rvr-horserescue.org/

STAY TUNED for the next installment! "Like" SHIRLEY ALARIE on Facebook or sign up for updates on SHIRLEYALARIE.COM

ABOUT THE AUTHOR

Shirley Alarie spent the first twenty years of her career in an industrial manufacturing environment, running around the hamster wheel as fast as her legs would carry her. A breast cancer diagnosis jammed on the brakes and forced her to put life in perspective. Shirley's journey since cancer has been focused on making a positive difference in the world, and she chose writing as her instrument to leave her mark.

Her *Lemons to Lemonade Series* serves meaningful and inspirational true stories in an engaging way. Shirley is currently underway on the third installment.

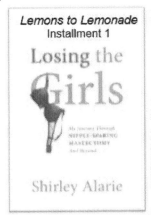

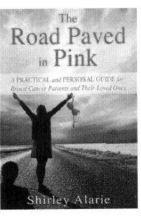

48018875R00132

Made in the USA
Charleston, SC
23 October 2015